Innovative Infrastructure Finance

Can Chen · John R. Bartle

Innovative Infrastructure Finance

A Guide for State and Local Governments

palgrave macmillan

Can Chen
Andrew Young School of Policy Studies
Georgia State University
Atlanta, GA, USA

John R. Bartle
College of Public Affairs and Community Service
University of Nebraska at Omaha
Omaha, NE, USA

ISBN 978-3-030-91410-3 ISBN 978-3-030-91411-0 (eBook)
https://doi.org/10.1007/978-3-030-91411-0

This Palgrave Macmillan imprint is published by the registered company Springer Nature Switzerland AG
The registered company address is: Gewerbestrasse 11, 6330 Cham, Switzerland

Can Chen dedicates this book to the memory of his father—Chen Helong who taught him to be an independent and determined person.

John R. Bartle dedicates this book to his wife, Lori Elliott-Bartle, with much love and admiration.

Preface

We all use infrastructure every day: to get to work (or to work from home using our Internet connection), for electricity and heating in our homes, drinking water, to flush our toilets, make phone calls, or send text messages. We rely on infrastructure for others to deliver goods to us and long-distance travel for business or pleasure. Public buildings house most schools and universities, libraries, many sports arenas, entertainment venues, as well as incarceration facilities. Many of us were born in government hospitals and have some of our happiest childhood memories in public parks. The symbols and tourist destinations of great cities are often monuments, bridges, stadiums, and public buildings. Reliable infrastructure is easy to take for granted until it fails and disrupts our lives in annoying and potentially dangerous ways.

Behind physical infrastructure is a network of people maintaining and improving it. Further in the background are those planning and financing it. Without good planning and financing, communities will inevitably crumble. Insufficient maintenance causes potholes, bridge failures, electrical outages, and contamination of drinking water. Poor planning and financing give us facilities that are "white elephants," or are too small, too expensive, or that do not anticipate technological or regulatory changes and are quickly rendered obsolete. Good infrastructure management is often the difference between a prosperous city and one in decline.

Infrastructure financing is changing rapidly. Innovations in finance present new options from simple to complex. We seek to demystify these options to give government officials and other interested citizens an understanding of the choices involved. New sources of funds can be used to fund capital projects, but more importantly, financing sources can be better matched with projects to create sustainable linkages between payments and benefits. Further, there are changes in what people want their cities to look like and which services they want governments to provide. The private sector is more involved in providing and financing infrastructure, and environmental and social goals are woven into financing tools. There are many opportunities to finance infrastructure in new ways. This book identifies these options and gives the reader a broad set of cases to help them take the next steps in bringing these innovations to their communities.

Innovation by its nature is hard to keep up with. We expect the topics and tools discussed here to change over time and vary from place to place. This book is not the last word on innovative financing options. It is a summary of current practice that shows several future paths for governments looking to improve their public assets and how they are financed.

As we finish this book, President Biden has just signed the Infrastructure Investment and Jobs Act which supporters say will be on par with historic federal initiatives such as the Interstate Highway System and the New Deal. Done right, the investment will, as President Biden says, "grow the economy, enhance our competitiveness, create good jobs, and make our economy more sustainable, resilient, and just." Done wrong, it will waste billions of dollars. This book is a playbook to help government managers get it done right.

Atlanta, GA, USA — Can Chen
Omaha, NE, USA — John R. Bartle

Acknowledgments

We owe thanks to Tula Weis, Thangasasan Boopalan, and Susan Westendorf of Palgrave Macmillan/Springer Nature Publishing for their effort and patience in seeing this book to completion. We also appreciate the input of three anonymous reviewers who reviewed the initial proposal.

Joshua Franzel of the International City/County Management Association provided us with instrumental survey data and feedback on earlier research that led to this book.

Several of our colleagues provided support and advice throughout this project, and at other times: Carol Ebdon and Craig Maher of the University of Nebraska at Omaha, Kenneth Kriz at the University of Illinois—Springfield, and Howard A. Frank, Shaoming Cheng, Hai (David) Guo of Florida International University, and Sally Wallace, Cathy Yang Liu, Gregory B. Lewis, W. Bartley Hildreth, and Ross Rubenstein at Georgia State University.

We appreciate many of our fellow researchers who produced excellent research that we have referenced here. We are also especially appreciative of many practitioners who patiently explained to us the projects they are involved in to share them with you. Their willingness to take on innovative projects to improve their community makes them the silent heroes of this book.

Acknowledgements

About This Book

This book is about innovation. While we celebrate entrepreneurs who take a chance and succeed, too often, we punish those who are not immediately successful when they experience some bumps in the road. It is unfortunate because we can learn from unsuccessful innovations and do it better the next time. As Nancy Matthews Elliott, the mother of Thomas Edison, said, "Never get discouraged if you fail. Learn from it. Keep trying."

Innovation in a complex field like public infrastructure finance can be more challenging than most. Besides learning and doing something new, the innovator needs to explain complex arrangements to elected officials and the public who will understand and support it. Americans are often skeptical of government, especially when it comes to money, and if they do not understand it, they are unlikely to support it. However, avoiding the challenge is not an acceptable alternative. Suitable investments create wealth, and equitable distribution of the benefits and burdens of capital development is necessary for a good and prosperous society.

In facing these challenges, state and local practitioners learn from each other. The goal of this book is to facilitate this sharing of knowledge. We describe many new financing alternatives. None of them are perfect, but all have worked somewhere and are worth considering. We review both successes and failures. A situation's context is critical to an innovation's feasibility; however, none of these innovations are guaranteed to work, but some might.

Chapter 1 of this book begins by defining infrastructure and explaining government involvement in providing these assets. Mayors and governors consistently identify infrastructure finance as one of their most significant challenges. We examine the trends in financing responsibilities among governments and the trends in spending in different sectors and find that funding is on a long-term decline. While the federal government may deliver a major injection of funds for state and local infrastructure, it is only a one-time solution to a long-term problem, even if this is fully funded.

Chapter 2 explains capital improvement plans and capital budgets used by state and local governments. It identifies three major new challenges facing governments in these areas: the increasing frequency of natural disasters, the opportunities and challenges of new technology, and the urgent priority to address social inequity in the provision of infrastructure finance.

Chapter 3 describes traditional methods of financing infrastructure, while Chapter 4 describes several innovative methods. We see these different methods as complementary—often, governments will do best by using some of each type. Many capital projects are big enough that one source of financing is not enough, nor will it match revenues appropriately with spending. Rather than being "either/or" decisions, a balance usually comes from mixing and matching funding sources that vary from one project to another.

Chapter 5 presents an in-depth look at six types of innovative financing. Each section describes the tool and then presents two or more case studies that vividly illustrate its use. Not all cases are successes, but all provide lessons that will help the reader decide whether and how to implement the tool in their community. Chapter 6 summarizes the lessons learned from all the cases and provides advice on implementing these innovative practices.

We hope this book will be helpful to both current and future practitioners. As Edison said, "The value of an idea lies in the using of it."

Contents

About the Authors

Can Chen is an Associate Professor in the Andrew Young School of Policy Studies at Georgia State University. His main research interest is state and local infrastructure finance and policy. He serves as the chair for the American Society of Public Administration (ASPA) Section on Transportation Policy and Administration (STPA) for 2021–2023. He is a certified research associate at Mineta Transportation Institute. His Bachelor's degree is from Harbin Engineering University, MPA from Xiamen University, and Ph.D. from the University of Nebraska at Omaha. He has published widely in journals on public budgeting and finance, public management and policy, and transportation. His research was supported by grant funding from the Governmental Accounting Standards Board (GASB), International City/County Management Association (ICMA), Lincoln Institute of Land Policy, and Open Government Partnership. He is the Associate Editor in *Journal of Infrastructure, Policy and Development* (JIPD) and *International Review of Public Administration* (IRPA), and the Public Budgeting and Finance Section Editor in *Chinese Public Administration Review* (CPAR).

John R. Bartle is the Dean of the College of Public Affairs and Community Service at the University of Nebraska at Omaha and a Professor of Public Administration and Urban Studies. He is a Fellow of the National Academy of Public Administration, a Congressionally chartered advisory group to the federal government. He is the co-author or editor of three other books: *Management Policies in Local Government Finance*, *Sustainable Development* *for Public Administration*, and *Evolving Theories of Public Budgeting*. His Bachelor's degree is from Swarthmore College, MPA from the University of Texas, Ph.D. from The Ohio State University, and an honorary Doctorate of Humane Letters from the State University of New York. He worked in city and state government in Minnesota and for state and national research organizations on tax policy issues. He leads an initiative to provide policy research for the Nebraska state legislature.

List of Figures

List of Tables

1

The Challenges and Opportunities of Financing Infrastructure

This chapter presents the context of funding and financing infrastructure in the U.S. The first section introduces the topic of infrastructure finance and provides an overview of the book structure. The second section provides the definition and scope of infrastructure. The key characteristics of infrastructure are described in the third section. The fourth section examines the trends and patterns in state and local infrastructure spending. The last section concludes with the core challenges and opportunities of infrastructure finance in the U.S.

1.1 Introduction

U.S. state and local governments play a central role in funding, operating, and maintaining transportation facilities, drinking water and sewer systems, public utilities, and telecommunications networks. However, state and local governments across the nation face a severe infrastructure deficit and are struggling to find new ways to finance needed expansions, upgrades, and repairs (Chen & Bartle, 2017).

Elected officials repeatedly mention infrastructure as a high priority. In their State of the City speeches in 2020, 63% of U.S. city mayors highlighted infrastructure issues, specifically roads and streets, water supply and wastewater, sidewalks, and transit (National League of Cities [NLC], 2020). In 2021, an NLC survey found infrastructure to be the top priority for mayors,

C. Chen and J. R. Bartle, *Innovative Infrastructure Finance*,
https://doi.org/10.1007/978-3-030-91411-0_1

with roads and bridges the most commonly cited type of infrastructure declining in quality. The primary factor of concern was insufficient funding, expressed by 91% of those surveyed (NLC, 2021). Similarly, a 2019 survey of 119 mayors of cities with a population over 75,000 by Boston University (2019) found infrastructure was the top challenge confronting mayors. The top three infrastructure priorities mentioned in the survey were roads (66%), water, wastewater, and stormwater (51%), and mass transit (43%). In their 2020 "state of the state" messages, governors focused on transportation infrastructure needs, including increasing spending, providing adequate funding for future needs, and broader transportation options, including public transit (National Association of State Budget Officers, 2020).

Meeting the infrastructure financing challenge has emerged as one of the most urgent issues facing the country. It is anticipated that federal legislation will help meet these needs and stimulate the economy; however, this does not eliminate the need for long-term financial solutions. Traditional sources of funding need to be supplemented by innovative sources. The requirement is not only for more money but to develop the right assets in the right places to contribute to long-term and sustainable growth. Frankel and Wachs (2017, p. 8) appropriately identify the core problem as a governance issue: "Problems that are presented as technological inadequacies or funding shortfalls arise primarily because of failures related to governance. These funding and management issues will not be resolved until governance and decision-making are improved but our current institutions seem structured to resist the necessary changes." Thus, in addition to funding, other parts of the solution are institutional governance and management.

Opening the institutions of governance to innovative approaches in managing and funding public assets is, therefore, a necessary step. Some state and local governments are already several steps ahead on this path. This book attempts to identify these creative steps to help other public managers consider appropriately developing and financing infrastructure for their communities. The book is organized as follows:

- In the remainder of this chapter, we define infrastructure, explain the rationale for public involvement, examine trends in spending, and identify government's challenges and opportunities. We find that:
  - State and local government spending on infrastructure is at its lowest percentage in 45 years.
  - Highways and streets are the largest category of infrastructure spending, followed by electric power, water supply, sewerage, and transit. Smaller

  amounts are spent on airports, water transportation, parking facilities, solid waste, and gas supply.
  - Many local government officials are concerned that available funding is insufficient to sustain even baseline maintenance of capital and that this shortfall adversely affects the community's quality of life.

- Chapter 2 describes the process of capital planning and budgeting used by state and local governments, discusses how citizens are involved in the process, and identifies new challenges presented by climate change, technology, and the demand for racial and gender equity.
- Chapter 3 describes traditional methods of financing infrastructure such as taxes, user charges, capital reserves, grants, and debt. These are the foundation of capital financing which new financing methods can supplement.
- Chapter 4 describes three types of innovative infrastructure financing:
  - New funding sources,
  - New financing mechanisms, such as credit assistance (loans, loan guarantees, and lines of credit) and alternative debt financing tools, and
  - New financial arrangements that engage new partners (the private sector, the nonprofit sector, or the general public) to participate in infrastructure financing and project delivery.
- Chapter 5 provides in-depth case analyses of six different types of innovative financing to illustrate best practices of government innovation and the lessons learned from each innovation to help government managers who are considering using these infrastructure financing options.
- Chapter 6 concludes by summarizing the lessons learned and identifies a path forward for innovation.

The creativity and innovation of government managers in this area provide new opportunities to fund infrastructure and engage the private sector to grow community wealth, enhance sustainability, and provide more equitable access to all. Governments should continue to use traditional sources to finance their investments. Still, there is an exciting opportunity to expand and enhance innovative financing methods to add to the toolkit of financial and capital managers.

We wrote this book to help government practitioners learn from their peers and better understand the widening variety of emerging financing mechanisms. Context and timing are critical for successful innovation. We offer practical suggestions and lessons learned from government managers who have adopted and implemented innovative financing mechanisms hoping that these good ideas can be more broadly employed to improve American communities.

1.2 Definition and Scope of Infrastructure

Infrastructure is the foundation of modern economies and societies. A robust, efficient, and well-maintained infrastructure system is critical to support and sustain the nation's economy, improve quality of life, and strengthen global competitiveness. In general, there is no standard or agreed-upon definition of infrastructure according to the current usage of the term. Two approaches to defining infrastructure exist in the literature. One approach is a narrow definition and refers to infrastructure as physical assets to support economic development. For example, the 2016 *Economic Report of the President* defines infrastructure as "fixed capital assets that are consumed jointly in various production processes that facilitate and support economic activities" (U.S. Council of Economic Advisers, 2016, p. 252). Under this definition, infrastructure comprises roads, bridges, tunnels, airports, transit, ports, parking, cycling and pedestrian infrastructure, railways, electric and gas utility production facilities and distribution networks, telecommunication systems, water and sewer systems, pollution control facilities, and solid waste management (see Table 1.1).

Another approach is a broader definition that regards infrastructure as a wide array of physical assets required to support both private economic activity and social services (U.S. Congressional Budget Office, 2008; U.S. Congressional Budget Office and Joint Committee on Taxation, 2009). According to this definition, infrastructure contains economic infrastructure and encompasses social infrastructure essential for a society to function. Social infrastructure includes schools, universities, hospitals, courts, correctional facilities, parks and recreational facilities, libraries, public buildings, and facilities (see Table 1.1).

These definitions are not without controversy. During the 2021 Congressional debate on the infrastructure bill, there was an intense debate over which definition of infrastructure was most appropriate. Behind this debate was political maneuvering by members of Congress to fund their favored projects. But it also surfaced legitimate philosophical differences about the appropriate role of government. Should funding prioritize economic development or social development? Where should new infrastructure be located, and which constituents have the highest need? These are questions for each political entity to decide. These decisions are both technical and political. Elected officials and citizens need to be involved in making these decisions, but appointed officials can provide critical advice about options and trade-offs in timing, location, and financing.

Table 1.1 Types and components of infrastructure

Economic Infrastructure	Social Infrastructure
Transportation Sector	*Education Sector*
Surface transportation (e.g., roads, bridges, railroads, parking)	Elementary schools and facilities
Public transit (e.g., urban rail, bus rapid transit)	University buildings and facilities
Aviation (airports, navigation aid systems)	*Public Health*
Water transportation (e.g., inland and seaports)	Healthcare facilities
Environmental Sector	Hospitals
Water supply and treatment (drinking)	*Judicial and Correctional Facilities*
Wastewater treatment (sewerage)	Prisons and jails
Solid waste management	Court houses
Pollution control facilities	*Housing and Community Development*
Utility Sector	Community centers
Electric power systems	*Government Buildings and Facilities*
Gas supply	City halls
Renewable energy infrastructure	Public safety and welfare facilities
Telecommunication and Digital Sector	*Civic and Cultural Buildings*
Telephone lines and networks	Libraries
High-speed internet	Convention centers
5G wireless network	*Parks and Recreation*

Source The Authors

Infrastructure projects have two key features that make their financing different from the daily operations of governments. The first feature is the large, up-front investments required for significant capital outlays. The second feature is the long economic life of the infrastructure assets. Due to the large capital outlay and the long-time horizon, infrastructure projects often present important risks, as a community that errs in the choice, design, and financing of a capital facility may have to live with it for a long time. This makes efficient and prudent infrastructure financing critically important. More broadly, bad federal and state incentives can lead to the construction of the wrong capital in the wrong places, leading to waste, congestion, and unsustainable development.

1.3 Public Goods and Benefits-Based Revenues

The traditional rationale for the public provision and infrastructure regulation is built upon the economic concepts of public goods and market failure. Infrastructure assets often produce public goods and services that are non-rival in consumption (several people can consume the same good simultaneously, such as public safety) and are non-excludable in use (exclusion from consumption is practically difficult, such as clean water). Goods and services that are non-rival and non-excludable are known as public goods (such as national defense). Private goods are the opposite: rival in consumption and excludable. Toll goods are non-rival but excludable (such as uncrowded toll roads or water supply that is not at capacity), and common pool goods are rival but non-excludable (such as congested streets or infinite groundwater supply). Many public assets also exhibit natural monopoly because their high fixed costs cause the per unit cost to decrease as production increases, such as subways and electric utilities. Many infrastructure assets also yield positive spillovers that are hard to monetize, such as parks or public health (Weimer & Vining, 2011). Public goods, toll goods, and common pool goods tend to be underprovided by private markets. This justifies public provision of these services and perhaps public ownership of the assets. Governments may also provide infrastructure for other reasons, such as equity considerations or economic development.

One of the principles of equity in finance identified by Adam Smith (1776, 1937) is the "benefits received" principle: People should provide financial support in proportion to their benefit from the public service. Infrastructure is well suited for benefits-based charges as many of the services offered are like private market transactions because services are provided to specific users. And, by its nature, infrastructure is place-specific, so the beneficiaries are often in identifiable political jurisdictions. Good investments also need to be of the right size and type, which will differ from one place to another. They may need to be culturally appropriate; for example, a public building can be a treasured asset or an eyesore depending partly on cultural norms that may value different architectural styles. Also, they need to be available and accessible for all to ensure equity for all users.

A recent application of Smith's benefits received principle is the benefit theory articulated by Dennis Young. While his focus is on nonprofit organizations, some of the insights are relevant to infrastructure. "The trick to successful financing, therefore, is to identify those benefits and beneficiaries and then determine what kind of transactions are best suited to effecting the exchange of benefits for financial or other types of income support" (Young,

2017, p. 41). A financial strategy should identify the beneficiaries of publicly provided services or assets and employ specific revenue sources to link the benefits and revenues. The nature of the good defines the appropriate revenue source:

- Infrastructure that provides private goods, such as drinking water, can be funded by charges and fees.
- Public goods, such as public streets, bike paths, and sidewalks, are best funded by taxes. If they enhance property value, then the property tax can be particularly appropriate.
- Toll goods that provide broad benefits but are excludable (such as libraries, parks, or swimming pools) can use charges and fees as part of their financing portfolio, as well as tax revenue. Special access can be provided to affinity groups (such as special events at the park or special library services) and people paying membership fees such as "Friends of the Park" or "Friends of the Library" groups.
- Exchange goods are publicly provided private goods that businesses are willing to support because of its public recognition or prestige, such as stadiums, convention centers, or buildings or spaces within colleges, airports, or public plazas.

This approach is more likely to create a sustainable flow of revenues because there is a logical connection between revenues and services. Owners of public assets should avoid "leaving money on the table," that is, providing benefits to users who could pay but are not asked to do so (Young, pp. 233–234). A careful inventory of the benefits provided and the degree to which specific revenue sources support them can identify opportunities to grow revenues.

Figure 1.1 shows the varying roles of the public and private sectors in the provision of different kinds of infrastructure assets in 2014. The public sector is the sole source of infrastructure investment for passenger railroads and public safety. It accounts for over three-quarters of infrastructure investment on mass transit and highways and streets. The public sector also supplies over half of infrastructure investment in educational facilities and buildings, aviation, and water transportation. In contrast, the private sector provides all investment in freight railroads and telecommunications and funds most of the investment in energy, healthcare facilities and hospitals, and amusement and recreational facilities.

In the U.S., infrastructure financing is a shared responsibility across different levels of government. As indicated in Fig. 1.2, state and local

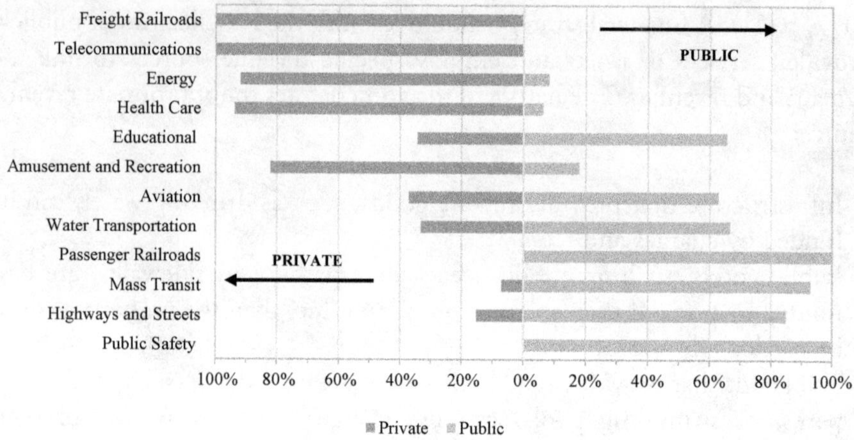

Fig. 1.1 Public and private share of investment in infrastructure, 2014 (*Data source* U.S. Bureau of Economic Analysis, 2015)

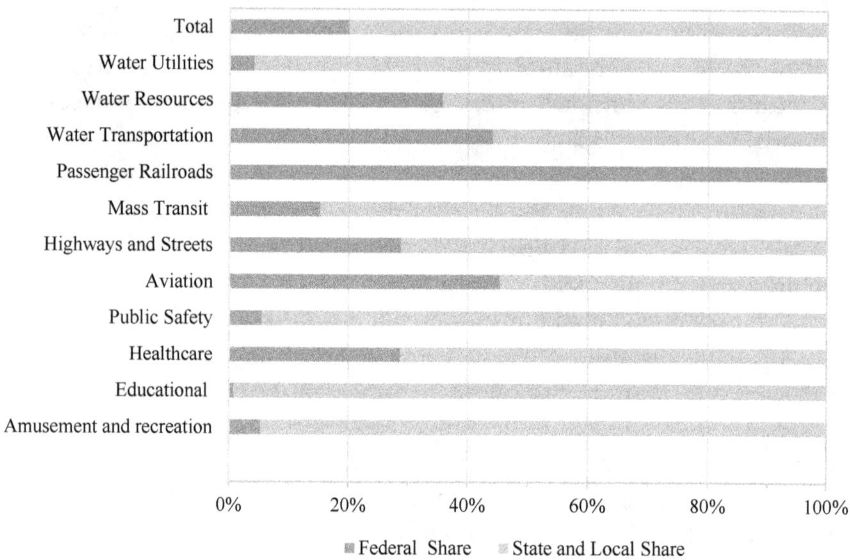

Fig. 1.2 Share of Infrastructure Investment by Levels of Government, 2014 (*Data source* U.S. Bureau of Economic Analysis, 2015)

governments are the primary provider and operators of core economic infrastructure; they fund most of the nation's roads, highways, transit systems, drinking water, and wastewater systems. In addition, they play a dominant role in funding several social infrastructure sectors such as public safety, educational facilities and buildings, health care, and amusement and recreation. The federal government is solely responsible for passenger railroads. It accounts for a relatively large role (over one-third) in funding aviation, water transportation, and water resources (e.g., dams, levees, reservoirs).

1.4 Trends in State and Local Infrastructure Financing

To analyze infrastructure spending trends, we focused on the core economic public infrastructure (as defined earlier). Figure 1.3 shows the state and local infrastructure spending trends by type of government from 1972 to 2017. In 1972, state and local infrastructure spending was $286 billion (in real 2012 dollars). Infrastructure spending rose substantially in 1977 and then fell in real terms in 1982. From 1982 to 1992, state and local infrastructure spending rose significantly and peaked in 1992 at $578 billion. Infrastructure spending then fell again between 1992 and 2002. There was modest growth in infrastructure spending from 2002 to 2017, but the amount of current infrastructure spending is still below the real spending level in 1992. The share of total state and local spending on infrastructure peaked at 32% in 1977 but then dropped precipitously to 21% in 1982. In 1992 there was an uptick, followed by a steady decrease since then to 13%.

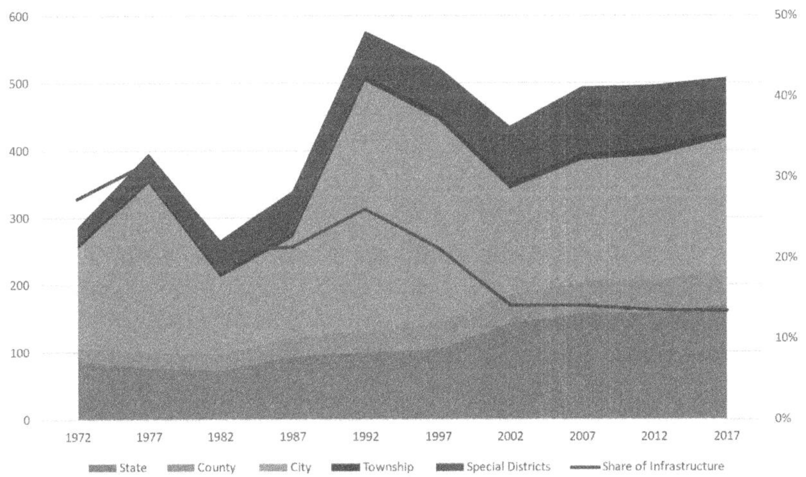

Fig. 1.3 State and local infrastructure spending by type of government 1972–2017 (*Note* The left axis is billions of real 2012 dollars. The right axis is the share of total state and local spending on infrastructure. *Data source* U.S. Census Bureau, Census of Governments, State and Local Government Finance [select years])

Turning to the amounts and shares of infrastructure spending by different types of governments, cities account for the largest amount and share of state and local infrastructure spending. In 1972, cities spent $148 billion on infrastructure, representing 52% of total state and local infrastructure expenditures. The highest level of real city infrastructure spending ($370 billion) was in 1992, representing 64% of total state and local infrastructure spending. Real city spending fell to $185 billion in 2012 and increased slightly to $195 billion in 2017, which accounted for 40% of total state and local infrastructure expenditures. States account for the second largest amount of state and local infrastructure spending. This amount has grown in real terms since 1982 and now represents over one-third of the state and local total. Together, cities and states are the main infrastructure owners, comprising 75% of total state and local infrastructure spending.

Special districts account for the third largest amount of state and local infrastructure spending. Special districts experienced steady growth in the amount of real infrastructure spending from 1972 to 2007. Spending grew from $24 billion in real terms in 1972, representing 8.4% of total state and local infrastructure expenditures, to $98 billion, representing 19.7% in 2007. Since 2007, real spending by special districts dropped to $77 billion, and the share of state and local spending was 15.2% in 2017.

In 1972, county governments spent $20 billion in real terms on local infrastructure, amounting to 7% of total state and local infrastructure spending. County infrastructure spending grew at a slow but steady pace throughout this period. In 2017, county governments spent $51 billion in real terms on infrastructure, accounting for 10% of state and local infrastructure expenditures. Township governments account for the smallest amount of infrastructure spending. Real spending grew from $7 billion in 1972 to $13 billion in 2017. Its share remained relatively stable at around 2.5%.

Figure 1.4 shows the composition of state and local infrastructure spending from 1972 to 2017. These data show the volatility of spending on these functions. The top five infrastructure spending categories are highways and streets, water supply, sewerage, electric power, and transit.

In 1972, state and local governments spent 48% of the infrastructure budget on highways and streets. Real dollar spending on this function was the same in 1997, with the share of total infrastructure spending dropping to 25.6%. Real spending rose from $134 billion in 1997 to $191 billion in 2017, with the share of spending rising to 37.5%.

Spending on water supply infrastructure saw a dramatic increase from 1982 to 1997, when it more than tripled in real terms from $30 billion to $99 billion, increasing its share from 11.2 to 18.8%. Since then, real spending

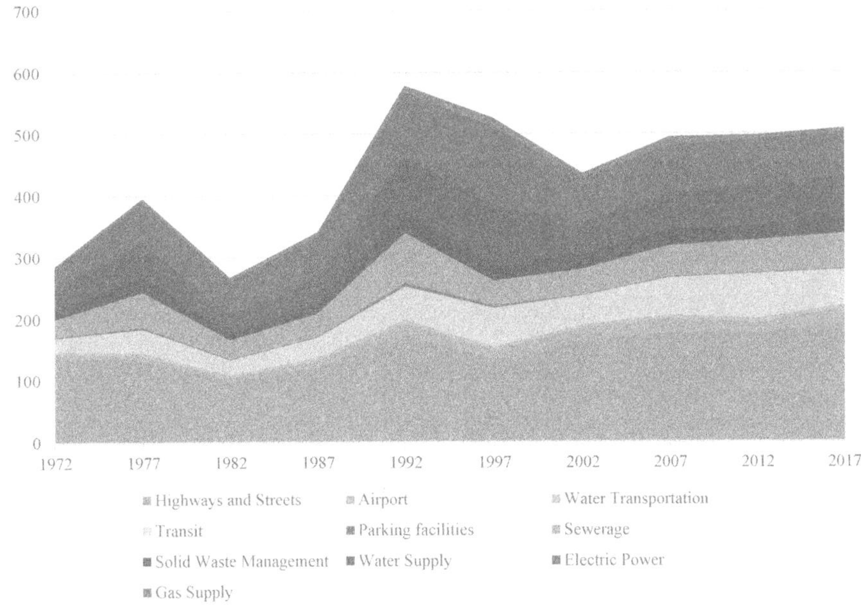

Fig. 1.4 State and local infrastructure spending by category of infrastructure 1972–2017 (*Note* The left axis is billions of 2012 dollars. *Data source* U.S. Census Bureau, Census of Governments, State and Local Government Finance [select years])

has not approached the 1997 level, with the percentage of spending at 13.3% in 2017. Spending on sewerage peaked at 14% of the state and local total in 1977, and now is 11% of the total.

Electric power spending has also been volatile, jumping from $29 billion in 1972 (10% of total infrastructure spending) to $128 billion in real terms in 1997, 24.3% of the total. By 2017, real spending fell to $72 billion or 14.2% of total infrastructure spending. Spending on transit has also fluctuated, growing from $21 billion in real terms (7.5%) in 1972, tripling to $64 billion in 1997 (12.2%). The trend since then has been variable, ranging from a share of 11% to almost 15%. The share of infrastructure spending on airports has risen from 1.7% in 1977 to 4.9% in 2017. The share of infrastructure spending on most of the other functions shown here has remained relatively constant. Gas supply had dropped from 2.7% in 2007 to 1.1% in 2017.

Figure 1.5 shows the state and local infrastructure spending composition by type of government from 1972 to 2017. State governments account for the largest portion of infrastructure spending on roads. Cities are the primary financing source for many types of infrastructure: airports, sewerage, electric power, water supply, gas supply and, solid waste. Special districts are the

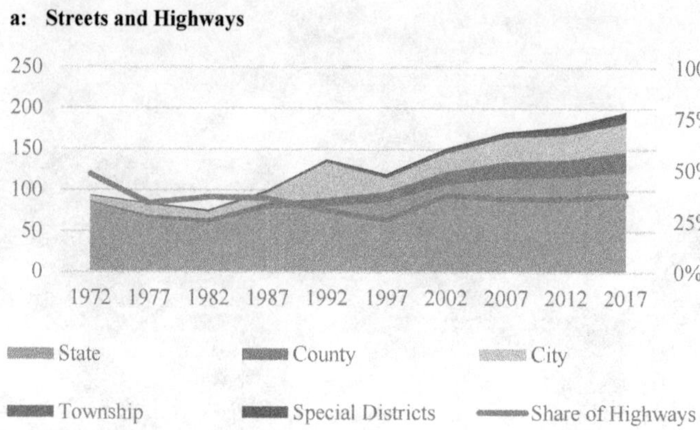

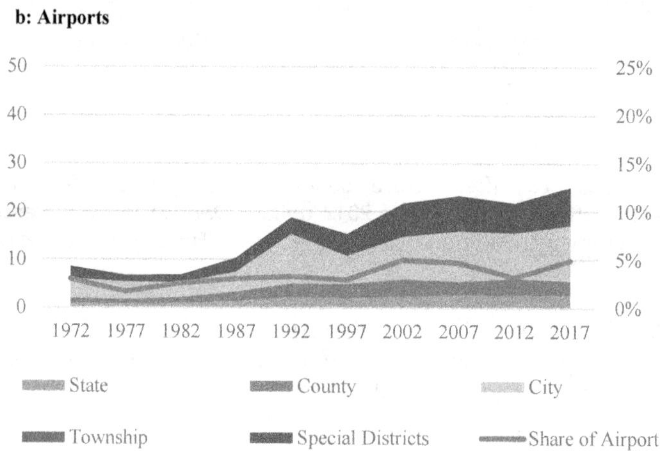

Fig. 1.5 Infrastructure spending by type of government and category of infrastructure 1972–2017. (**a**) Streets and Highways; (**b**) Airports; (**c**) Water Transportation; (**d**) Transit; (**e**) Sewerage; (**f**) Solid Waste Management; (**g**) Water Supply; (**h**) Electric Power; (**i**) Gas Supply (*Note* The left axis is in billions of 2012 dollars. The right axis is the share of total state and local infrastructure spending on that function. *Data source* U.S. Census Bureau, Census of Governments, State and Local Government Finance [select years])

largest suppliers of funding for transit infrastructure and water transportation. The shares of state and local infrastructure spending on each function are shown in Figs. 1.5a–i.

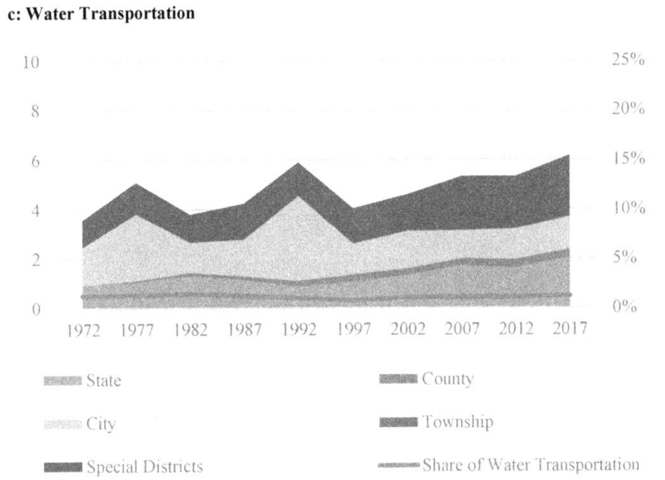

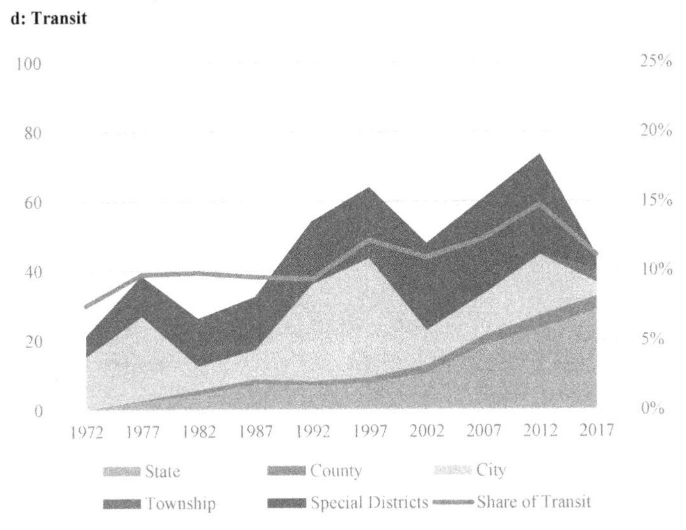

Fig. 1.5 (continued)

1.5 Challenges

Governments face significant challenges to the funding and provision of infrastructure and service in the future. According to a survey of 601 local government respondents by the International City/County Management Association (2017), nearly 42% believe that the jurisdiction's infrastructure needs additional funding to sustain even baseline maintenance and that the current state of local infrastructure adversely affects the community's quality

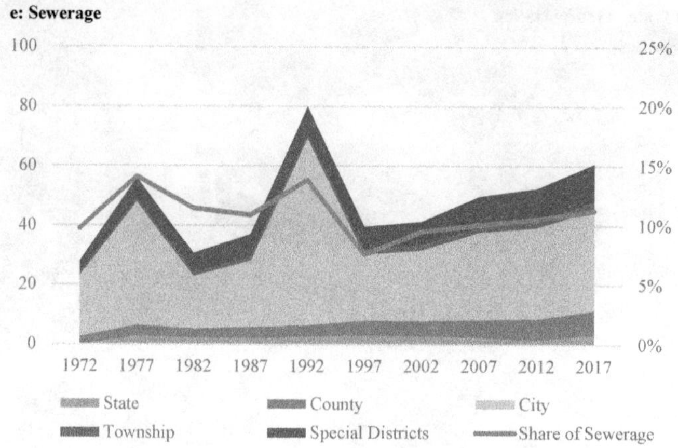

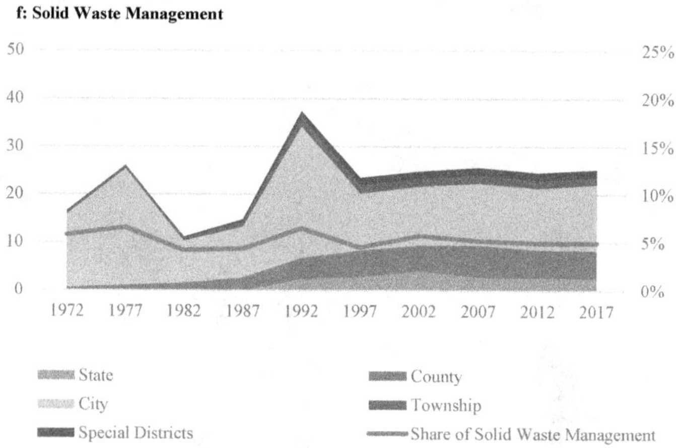

Fig. 1.5 (continued)

of life. In contrast, only 13% of local government respondents believe that the current state of the jurisdiction's infrastructure meets community needs and that adequate funding is available to maintain and develop the assets. In addition, 45% of respondents contend that local infrastructure improvements could be made, and additional infrastructure funding is preferred.

Many factors contribute to the current challenges of infrastructure financing. On the demand side, due to population growth and urbanization, government spending on infrastructure has not kept pace with the investment demands of the system. The number of cars per household has increased from 1.84 in 1984 to 1.96 in 2015, and the miles traveled per vehicle has increased from 6,612 in 1984 to 8,648 in 2015 (Sivak, 2017). The same is true for air

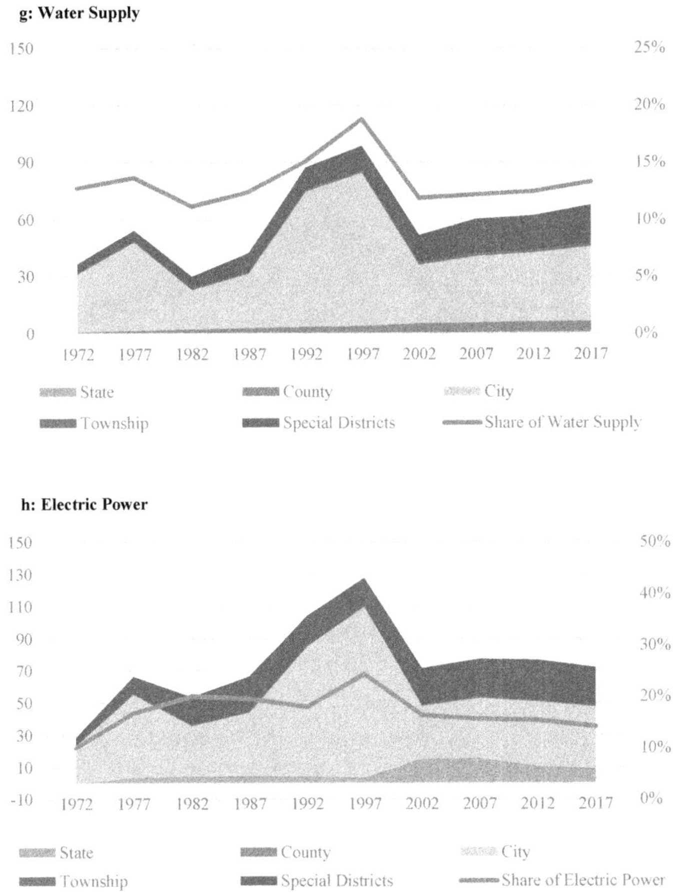

Fig. 1.5 (continued)

travel, freight traffic, and public transit, and these trends are projected to continue (Bartle & Chen, 2015). The American Society of Civil Engineers (ASCE) (2020) estimates that there is a $2 trillion, 10-year investment gap, which includes a $836 billion backlog for highway and bridge capital needs. The U.S. Environmental Protection Agency (EPA) (2013) has identified a total capital improvement need of $384 billion for investing in public water infrastructure systems over the next 20 years. Consequently, state and local governments face a major investment gap in funding infrastructure projects.

The demand for services is also increasing for several economic and social reasons. Climate change is creating a need for flood mitigation. Shifting supply chains puts demands on transportation networks to accommodate the increased movement of freight goods. Technological advancements are changing the vehicles we drive and the infrastructure to support them.

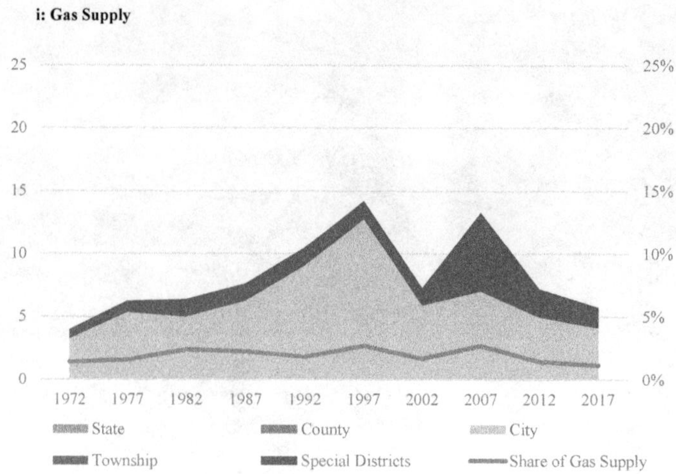

Fig. 1.5 (continued)

Younger people are demanding more livable urban spaces, which changes the urban form and transportation networks. Environmental sustainability requires infrastructure that uses less energy and encourages less wasteful decisions by users. And the urgent demand for greater social equity requires that access to the services provided by public assets be equal and fair.

On the supply side, rising capital construction costs, shrinking public infrastructure funding sources, and constrained public sector budgets due to rising health care and pension costs threaten the future sustainability of state and local infrastructure finance. According to the National League of Cities (2016) report, declining and unstable federal and state funding and increasing mandates have placed increasing pressure on local governments to finance infrastructure.

1.6 Opportunities

Despite these financial pressures, there are compelling opportunities. As Frankel and Wachs (2017, p. 6) wrote, "Infrastructure comprises a huge portion of our shared wealth, and it crosses political boundaries. Effectively managing and enhancing our collective assets are among the most pressing challenges to contemporary government and require actions beyond merely spending more money." This effective management of public assets is the key to addressing these challenges.

While the growth in demand presents a challenge, it indicates that more consumers are willing to pay for the services provided. For the many projects that meet the market test of profitability, individuals and businesses that will benefit from economic development spurred by infrastructure development should be willing to provide financial support if appropriate financial instruments are employed. One key goal is development that grows community wealth with as few of the problems of pollution and congestion as possible. While demands for greater environmental sustainability and racial and gender equity may seem to place greater demands on local officials, they are legitimate democratic expressions of how citizens want their communities to adjust. Elected and appointed officials who hear these demands and develop strategies to meet them will be successful leaders. The opportunity exists to create revenue streams to invest in public assets to facilitate long-term, sustainable economic growth. The financial instruments to create these assets are in use but need to be appropriately harnessed. This book provides a roadmap for the practitioner interested in meeting this challenge.

References

American Society of Civil Engineers (ASCE). (2020). *Infrastructure report card.* http://www.infrastructurereportcard.org. Accessed 20 August 2021.

Bartle, J. R., & Chen, C. (2015). Future issues in state transportation finance. In K. G. Willoughby & M. M. Rubin (Eds.), *Sustaining the states: The fiscal viability of American state governments* (pp. 211–234). Taylor & Francis Group Press.

Boston University. (2019). *Menino survey of mayors: 2019 results.* https://www.surveyofmayors.com/reports/Menino-Survey-of-Mayors-2019-Final-Report.pdf. Accessed 20 August 2021.

Chen, C., & Bartle, J. R. (2017). Infrastructure financing: A guide for local government managers. International City Management Association and Government Finance Officers Association. http://icma.org/en/Article/107858/Local_Governments_Explore_Alternative_Financing_to_Address_Infrastructure_Needs. Accessed 20 August 2021.

Frankel, E., & Wachs, M. (2017). More than money: Infrastructure and governance. *Public Works Management & Policy, 22*(1), 6–11.

Innovations and emerging practices in local government 2016 survey: Summary report of results. https://icma.org/sites/default/files/309068_ICMA%20Innovation%20Survey%20Summary%20Report.pdf. Accessed 1 August 2021.

National Association of State Budget Officers. (2020). *Summaries of governors' 2020 state of the state addresses.* https://higherlogicdownload.s3.amazonaws.com/NASBO/9d2d2db1-c943-4f1b-b750-0fca152d64c2/UploadedImages/Issue%20Briefs%20/SOS_Summary_2020.pdf. Accessed 20 August 2021.

National League of Cities. (2016). *Paying for local infrastructure in an era of federalism: A state-by-state analysis.* http://www.nlc.org/find-city-solutions/city-solutions-and-applied-research/infrastructure/local-infrastructure-funding-report. Accessed 20 August 2021.

National League of Cities. (2020). *State of the cities 2020.* https://www.nlc.org/resource/state-of-the-cities-2020/. Accessed 20 August 2021.

National League of Cities. (2021). *State of the cities 2021.* https://www.nlc.org/resource/state-of-the-cities-2021/. Accessed 20 August 2021.

Sivak. (2017). *Has motorization in the U.S. peaked? Part 9: Vehicle ownership and distance drivern, 1984 to 2015.* http://websites.umich.edu/~umtriswt/PDF/SWT-2017-4.pdf. Accessed 20 August 2021.

Smith, A. (1776, republished in 1937). *The wealth of nations.* New York: Random House.

U.S. Bureau of Census. (various years). *Census of governments, state and local government finance.*

U.S. Bureau of Economic Analysis. (2015). *National income and product accounts—Fixed assets.* http://www.bea.gov/iTable/index_FA.cfm. Accessed 20 August 2021.

U.S. Congressional Budget Office (2008). *Issues and options in infrastructure investment.* https://www.cbo.gov/sites/default/files/110th-congress-2007-2008/reports/05-16-infrastructure.pdf. Accessed 20 August 2021.

U.S. Congressional Budget Office and Joint Committee on Taxation. (2009). *Subsidizing infrastructure investment with tax-preferred bonds.* https://www.cbo.gov/sites/default/files/111th-congress-2009-2010/reports/10-26-taxpreferred bonds.pdf. Accessed 20 August 2021.

U.S. Council of Economic Advisers. (2016). *2016 economic report of the president.* https://www.whitehouse.gov/administration/eop/cea/economic-report-of-the-President/2016. Accessed 20 August 2021.

U.S. Department of Transportation. (2019). *Highway statistics, 2019.* https://www.fhwa.dot.gov/policyinformation/statistics/2019/. Accessed 20 August 2021.

U.S. Environmental Protection Agency. (2013). *Drinking water infrastructure needs survey and assessment.* https://www.epa.gov/sites/production/files/2015-07/documents/epa816r13006.pdf. Accessed 20 August 2021.

Weimer, D. L., & Vining, A. R. (2011). *Policy analysis: Concepts and practice.* Longman.

Young, D. R. (2017). *Financing nonprofits and other social enterprises: A benefits approach.* Edward Elgar.

2

Capital Planning and Budgeting for Infrastructure

In the U.S., state and local governments are responsible for maintaining and improving a substantial portion of our public infrastructure systems. Every year, state and local governments spend billions of dollars on building infrastructure that will be used for many years. Therefore, it is prudent to develop a long-term capital plan and budget to identify and prioritize capital needs, establish project scope and costs, estimate funding and financing sources, and project future operating and maintenance costs.

In this chapter, we present the rationale for having a capital plan and budget for state and local governments, describe the typical process of capital planning and budgeting, and discuss contemporary issues and challenges in capital planning and budgeting.

2.1 What Is a Capital Improvement Plan?

2.1.1 Define Capital Assets and Capital Expenditures

In 1999, the Governmental Accounting Standards Board (GASB, 1999) issued Statement No. 34, *Basic Financial Statements—And Management's Discussion and Analysis—For State and Local Governments* (GASB 34). GASB 34 represented a dramatic shift in the way state and local governments report and present capital assets. GASB 34 defines capital assets as either tangible or intangible assets that are used in the operations of governments and that have

C. Chen and J. R. Bartle, *Innovative Infrastructure Finance*,
https://doi.org/10.1007/978-3-030-91411-0_2

a useful life extending beyond one single reporting period (typically a year). There are many types of capital assets:

- Land and land improvements,
- Buildings and building improvements,
- Vehicles,
- Machinery and equipment,
- Works of art and historical treasures,
- Infrastructure, and
- Other tangible or intangible assets.[1]

The GASB defines infrastructure assets as "long-lived capital assets that normally are stationary in nature and normally can be preserved for a significantly greater number of years than most capital assets." Examples of infrastructure assets include roads, bridges, tunnels, drainage systems, water and sewer systems, dams, and lighting systems (GASB, 1999). One goal of GASB 34 is to help government officials "to understand the extent to which the government has invested in capital assets, including roads, bridges, and other infrastructure assets ... and a new and more comprehensive way to demonstrate their stewardship ... through the budget process" (GASB, 1999, p. 5). Each government has the flexibility to define its own threshold value for defining capital expenditures. Government outlays that fall below the threshold are not treated as capital projects.

2.1.2 Defining a Capital Improvement Plan (CIP) and Capital Budget

In state and local governments, long-term capital planning is usually conducted by a multi-year Capital Improvement Plan (CIP). A CIP is a blueprint for planning a community's public capital projects over a multi-year period (five or six years). It outlines capital project costs, funding sources, and estimated future operating and maintenance costs associated with each capital project (Bunch, 2012; Marlowe et al., 2009). CIPs are often reviewed and updated annually to reflect changing community needs, priorities, and

[1] In 2009, GASB issued Statement No. 51, "Accounting for intangible assets," to provide guidance for the accounting and financial reporting of intangible assets. GASB 51 describes the key characteristics of intangible assets: "lack of physical substance, nonfinancial nature (receivable or prepayments are not intangible assets), and initial useful life extends beyond a single reporting period." The common types of intangible assets include patents, copyrights, trademarks, easements, licenses, and computer software.

funding opportunities. A capital budget is a separate budget document from the operating budget document. It contains capital projects in the first and second years of the CIP, which are presented and approved by the governing body. The key difference between the capital budget and the CIP is that the projects in the capital budget are authorized by the governing body. However, the list of five or six-year capital projects in the CIP does not obligate the governing body to spend on these projects.

The development of a CIP and capital budget needs to be prepared within a broader context of state and local governments' visions, strategies, and priorities. Figure 2.1 depicts the integration of a CIP and capital budget with the government's plans.

2.2 Why Have a Capital Plan and Budget?

2.2.1 Rationale for a Capital Budget

Why do state and local governments consider capital projects separately? Capital expenditures are distinct from current spending for three reasons: (1) Capital projects are relatively expensive, and the funding and financing of capital projects are complex and often come from other sources. (2) Capital projects often take a long time to build, and so the funding needs to span more than one year. Once capital expenditures are made, they cannot be changed easily. (3) Capital assets are expected to provide service for many years and significantly impact future operating budgets. In sum, the size of the expenditure and the longevity of capital assets distinguish capital expenditures from operating spending. The vast majority of state and local governments distinguish capital from current spending in the form of either CIPs or capital budgets, or both.

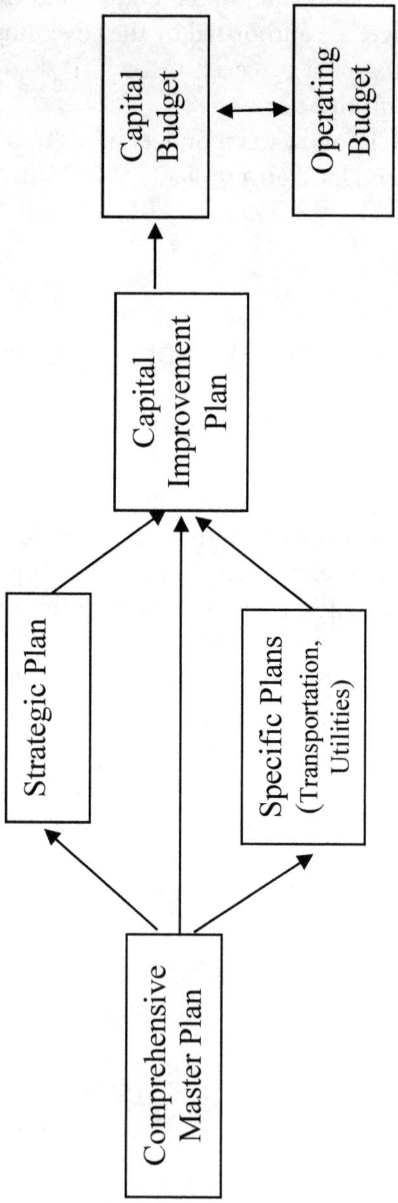

Fig. 2.1 The linkages between CIP and general government plans (*Source* The Authors)

2.2.2 The Benefits of Developing a Capital Plan and Budget

There are many significant benefits to a robust capital plan and budget, even for small local governments.[2] The key benefits are the following (Bunch, 2012; Marlowe et al., 2009; Mikesell, 2014):

- Link community strategic goals to prioritize community long-term capital investment,
- Facilitate coordination between capital needs and the impact on the operating budget,
- Enhance intra- and intergovernmental and cross-sectoral collaboration,
- Spread the costs of providing capital improvements over time, thereby stabilizing tax rates and creating more financial flexibility in the future,
- Help avoid costly, unnecessary, and duplicated capital projects,
- Improve the efficiency and cost-effectiveness of capital investment,
- Balance competing capital needs with limited fiscal resources,
- Make prudent funding and financing arrangements for capital projects,
- Inform the public and stakeholders about future capital needs and operating impacts,
- Ensure accountability for maintaining and upgrading public capital assets, and
- Maintain and improve the community's credit rating.

2.3 How to Develop a Capital Plan and Budget

2.3.1 The Policy Framework

State and local governments establish a formal policy framework for planning and budgeting capital projects. The policy framework usually includes the following important elements:

- Establish the goals and objectives of the capital plan and budget,
- Define what kinds of capital expenditures will be included in the capital plan and budget,

[2] The federal budget and budget process are unified, and the federal government does not have a separate capital budget process. Scholars and policymakers have long debated the merits of adopting a capital budget for the federal government (Mikesell 2014; Lee, Johnson, and Joyce 2021; U.S. Government Accountability Office [GAO], 1987; United States President's Commission to Study Capital Budgeting, 1999).

- Decide on a planning horizon for a CIP,
- Develop a timeline for creating the CIP and approve the capital budget,
- Determine who will lead and participate in the capital planning and budgeting process,
- Identify criteria for identifying and prioritizing capital projects, and
- Determine how to engage citizens in the capital planning and budgeting process.

Capital Budgeting in the City of Miami, Florida

- In the City of Miami, Florida, the Office of Management and Budget, and the Office of Capital Improvements jointly prepare for a capital improvements plan (CIP). The Miami's CIP is a comprehensive and six-year plan for repairing, maintaining, and improving city-owned public infrastructure assets.
- The City of Miami defines a capital improvement as "the acquisition, construction, reconstruction, or installation of a physical public improvement or an addition to fixed assets in the form of land, buildings, or improvements with a value of $5,000 or more and a useful life of at least three years" (The City of Miami, 2021, p. 6).
- The annual capital budget document is separate from the operating budget document. It refers to the first year of the six-year CIP and presents the detailed funding schemes for purchasing new land, buildings, or equipment and repairing and building major infrastructure projects. In addition, the CIP is arranged by departments. Each capital project belongs to a distinct capital program fund according to the attributes of the project: General government, public safety, disaster recovery, public facilities, parks and recreation, streets and sidewalks, mass transit, sanitary sewers, storm sewers, and solid waste.
- The City of Miami incorporates its strategic initiatives as the policy framework for developing a CIP. All requested capital projects, facilities, and equipment must meet one or more of the following strategic goals:
  - Enhancing the quality of life
  - Strengthening community resiliency
  - Promoting economic prosperity
- During the process of preparing for a CIP, the City of Miami uses the following sources to identify capital projects and needs:
  - Client departments identify and submit capital project requests.
  - External agencies (e.g., Downtown Development Authority, Community Redevelopment Agencies) identify and submit capital project requests.
  - Local mitigation strategy (LMS) demands capital projects to reduce or eliminate the long-term risk to human life and property from natural hazards.

- Collaborative capital projects with other government agencies (Miami-Dade County, the Florida Department of Transportation, and the U.S. Department of Transportation).

Source The City of Miami (2021). *FY 2022 Proposed Capital Budget*. http://archive.miamigov.com/Budget/docs/FY22/FY22ProposedCapital.pdf.

2.4 The Process of Capital Planning and Budgeting

Capital planning and budget processes vary considerably from one local government to another and from state to state. According to the National Association of State Budget Officers (NASBO)'s report—*Capital Budget Process in the States*, 43 states have a multi-year capital improvement plan, ranging from 3 to 10 years, 32 states have a capital budget document that is distinct from the operating budget, while 18 states have a capital budget that is included as part of the operating budget (NASBO, 2014). The state and local government process generally consists of five stages (Marlowe et al., 2009; Mikesell, 2014). Each of these stages is discussed in detail in the following sections (Fig. 2.2).

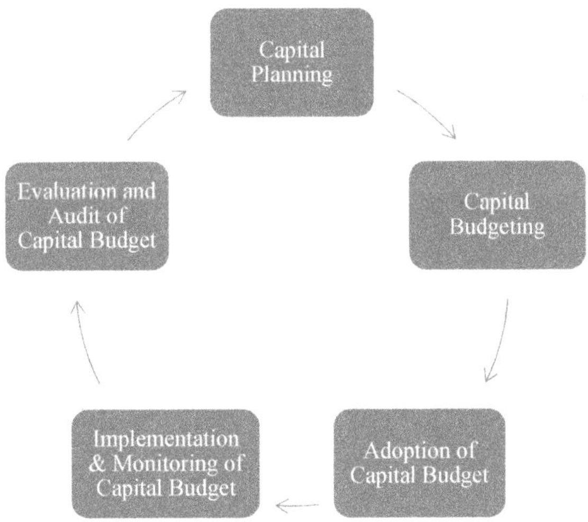

Fig. 2.2 The capital budget cycle (*Source* The Authors)

2.4.1 Capital Planning

Governments start their infrastructure development with a comprehensive capital planning effort which includes several elements. The first element is to estimate community capital needs which involve the following steps: (1) conduct an inventory of existing capital assets and assess current service characteristics, (2) estimate future service requirements using broader environmental trends, and (3) identify capital needs by determining service objectives. The key information in an inventory of capital assets includes age, degrees of usage, physical condition, service capacity, maintenance records, and estimated replacement cost. Such an inventory helps the government estimate needs for renewal, replacement, expansion, addition, and future maintenance of its capital stock.

After determining the inventory and estimated capital needs, the second element in capital planning is identifying and compiling a list of government agencies' capital projects. Typically, each proposed capital project includes a justification, estimated cost, and sponsor agencies. A government-wide planning department or commission may screen the preliminary list of capital project proposals. The third element is to evaluate and prioritize proposed capital projects. This element is critical to a successful multi-year capital plan. There are several important factors to consider when evaluating and ranking capital project requests, including (Mikesell, 2014; Office of the New York State Comptroller, 2009):

- Public health and safety concerns,
- Legal mandates by court order, state, or federal governments,
- Economic, environmental, or social issues and values of the community or region,
- Operational benefits to the government,
- Specific needs or demands for improved services, timeliness, or cost savings,
- Investment return (e.g., saving on maintenance),
- Capacity to leverage other resources (e.g., matching funds),
- Project feasibility (cost, time frames, management capacity), and
- Project risks.

Capital Project Prioritization Criteria in the City of Miami, Florida

- A project prioritization matrix with nine criteria is utilized by the City of Miami for ranking and prioritizing capital projects. Projects receiving the highest ranking are given priority funding and implementation in the City's CIP.
- The nine capital project prioritization criteria are the following:
  - Life, health, and safety
  - Legal and regulatory
  - Essential improvements
  - Strategic alignment
  - Infrastructure risk management and resilience
  - Environmental protection
  - Coordination and dependency
  - Leverage external funds
  - Revenue producing or cost saving.

Source The City of Miami. (2021). *FY 2022 Proposed Capital Budget*. http://archive.miamigov.com/Budget/docs/FY22/FY22ProposedCapital.pdf.

2.4.2 Capital Budgeting

Governments need to keep CIPs within their limited financial capacities. The second step of this process is to perform a budgetary and financial analysis. Three key efforts are contained in this step: (1) assess the financial capacity of the government, including the government's operating expenditure level, revenue capacity, debt service requirements, debt capacity, and available external funding, (2) forecast the budgetary impact of capital projects. The development of capital assets may have a significant impact on future operating budgets. It is crucial to offer reliable and accurate estimates of each capital project's budgetary impact on future operating budgets such as debt service costs, maintenance costs, and operating costs, and (3) make sound funding and financing arrangements for capital acquisition. Capital projects may be expensive and often involve debt finance. It is important to identify the most economical means of financing capital projects, ensure that the timing of the funding matches that of the project, and provide sufficient funding sources to repay the borrowed money as well as the operating and maintenance costs.

2.4.3 Adoption of Capital Budget

After all aspects of the capital project planning and budgeting (policies, needs, priorities, costs, and financing) have been addressed, the next step is to adopt the multi-year CIP formally. Once approved by local governing bodies or state legislatures, the first and perhaps second year of CIP becomes the legally adopted capital budget. In most cases, capital projects in the first and second years of CIP receive budgetary appropriations at that time. Before final adoption, state and local governments often seek public input on the proposed capital plan. Citizens, business leaders, and interest groups are given opportunities to review capital program priorities and voice any concerns (see Sect. 2.5).

2.4.4 Implementation and Monitoring of Capital Budget

The primary goals of capital budget implementation are to (1) determine if capital project goals meet the community's current and future needs and (2) routinely monitor approved capital projects and ensure they remain on schedule and within budget. Delay and cost overruns are common problems that create both management and political problems. While some delays and cost overruns are inevitable, state and local government officials need to keep the public and stakeholders informed about the status of capital projects and explain any problems that occur.

2.4.5 Evaluation and Audit of Capital Budget

The final step is the evaluation and audit of a capital budget. Upon completing the project and paying all expenses, the government needs to close out the capital project accounts. Audits of a capital budget serve three key goals: (1) ensure capital projects are in compliance with the provision of appropriation bills and ensure honesty in dispensing public monies, (2) prevent waste, and (3) evaluate the effectiveness of the capital programs.

2.5 Citizen Involvement in Capital Budgeting

Because capital projects often involve substantial costs and carry long-term implications, involving citizens in the capital planning and budgeting process is critical. Effective citizen input helps ensure that the capital projects selected are valued by the community and that citizens understand the need to assure the financial responsibility to finance these projects (Marlowe et al., 2009).

In practice, state statutes and local charters often require governments to seek public input to identify, review, and prioritize capital projects. There are a variety of methods of citizen involvement in the capital planning and budgeting process:

- Citizen survey and focus groups,
- Community forums,
- Neighborhood and civic association meetings,
- Online feedback, such as websites, comment forms, email boxes, and interactive dialogues,
- Social media (Facebook, Twitter, Next Door),
- Citizen committees and advisory groups,
- Individual or group emails, phone calls, and in-person contact, and
- Public hearings.

Public Engagement for Capital Projects in the Arlington County, Virginia

- The Arlington County, Virginia develops a guide of "A Six-Step Public Engagement Guide for Capital Project" to advance public engagement practices for capital budgeting.
- The detailed six steps for public engagement in capital projects are as follows:
  - Step 1: Clearly define the project
  - Step 2: Identify project stakeholders
  - Step 3: Determine level of engagement
  - Step 4: Create and implement engagement and communication strategies
  - Step 5: Conduct analysis for decision-makers
  - Step 6: Complete project closeout and after-action review.
- Seven public engagement values are prescribed in this public engagement guide:
  - Inclusion and mutual respect
  - Early involvement and timely communication
  - Transparent and accountable
  - Clear and accessible communication
  - Open, two-way communication
  - Fiscally sustainable
  - Continuous improvement.
- Four levels of public engagement for county capital projects are identified in this guide. They are:

- **Communicate**: Keep community informed on project updates, changes, regulatory constraints, and progress through the lifecycle of the project,
- **Consult**: Keep community informed, listen to views, and provide feedback on how the input influenced the project and/or decisions,
- **Involve**: Share how concerns were reflected in solutions and designs developed, and share how inputs influenced the final decision of project,
- **Collaborate**: Seek community input in partnership with stakeholders.

Source The County of Arlington, Virginia. (2018). *Six-Step Public Engagement Guide for Capital Projects.* https://arlingtonva.s3.dualstack.us-east-1.amazonaws.com/wp-content/uploads/sites/21/2018/03/Six-Step-Public-Engagement-Guide-for-Capital-Projects.pdf.

2.6 Emerging Challenges in Capital Planning and Budgeting

State and local governments face new challenges to infrastructure planning, including (1) climate change and the environment, (2) emerging technologies such as smart city infrastructure, connected, and autonomous vehicles and electric vehicles, and (3) planning more equitable infrastructure investment to address racial and gender inequities.

2.6.1 Climate Change and the Environment

Climate change is one of the greatest global challenges facing our society. It is defined as "a change of climate which is attributed directly or indirectly to human activity that alters the composition of the global atmosphere and which is in addition to natural climate variability observed over comparable time periods" (United Nation, 1992, p.7). Because of the dramatic climate change, natural disasters are occurring more frequently and are increasing severe. In the latest sixth global assessment, the Intergovernmental Panel on Climate Change (IPCC) concludes that global temperatures will rise beyond 1.5 °C and 2 °C during the twenty-first century and increased global warming will escalate the frequency and intensity of heat extremes, marine heatwaves, heavy precipitation, tropical cyclones, agricultural and ecological droughts (2021).

In the U.S., the Fourth National Climate Assessment contends that "climate change creates new risks and exacerbates existing vulnerabilities in communities across the U.S., presenting growing challenges to human health and safety, quality of life, and the rate of economic growth" (US Global Change Research Program, 2018, p. 25). According to National Oceanic and Atmospheric Administration (NOAA, 2021), the U.S. has experienced \$285 billion weather and climate disasters that have exceeded \$1.875 trillion in total damages since 1980. In 2020, the U.S. had a record-smashing 22 weather and climate disasters that killed at least 262 people and totaled approximately \$95 billion damage (Fig. 2.3). Climate change also poses growing challenges for all infrastructure sectors. In 2017, about 94.7 million people (30% of the U.S. population) lived in coastal areas, a 15.3% growth since 2000 (U.S. Census Bureau, 2019). As this number grows, critical infrastructure sectors (e.g., highways, seaports, and energy facilities) are increasingly vulnerable to climate impacts such as rising sea levels, storm surges, and flooding. Inland local communities also face similar problems of wildfires, flooding, and drought.

As climate change continues to worsen, political decision-makers have been frequently asking the question of how to make local communities and businesses more resilient to the changing climate. Infrastructure will be affected by the impacts of climate change but will also play an essential role in building resilience to the impacts of climate change. In its recent report, the Global Commission on Adaptation highlight that climate-resilient infrastructure systems are one of the top six areas of investment required to adapt to a

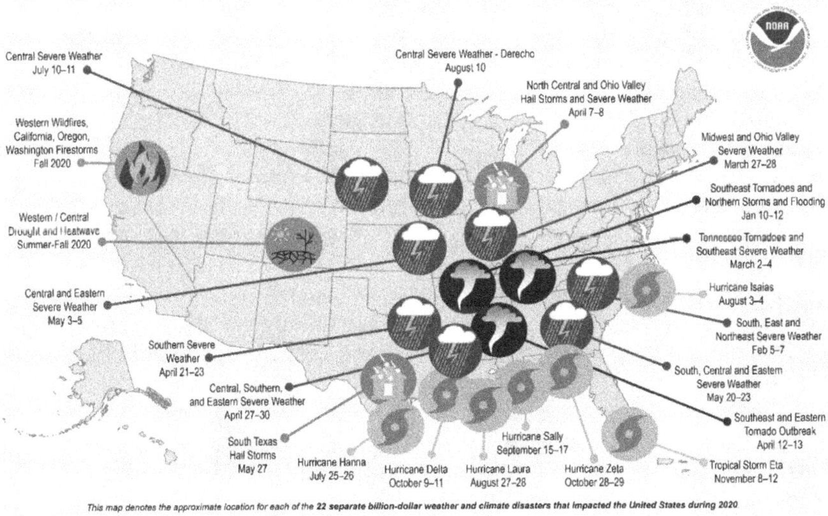

Fig. 2.3 U.S. 2020 billion-dollar weather and climate disasters (*Source* U.S. National Oceanic and Atmospheric Administration [NOAA] https://coast.noaa.gov/states/fast-facts/hurricane-costs.html)

climate-uncertain future and failing to ensure the climate resilience of infrastructure will have major economic consequences (The Global Commission on Adaptation, 2019). There are different estimates of the investment needs of climate-resilient infrastructure projects. The United Nations Environment Programme (UNEP) (2016) predicts the cost of adapting to climate change in developing countries could rise to between $280 and $500 billion per year by 2050. Based on the Global Commission on Economy and Climate, under a low-carbon scenario, by 2030, it was estimated the world needs $93 trillion in climate-resilient infrastructure by 2030 and 70% of this estimate relates to urban areas (Birch & Rodas, 2020). Recently, in the U.S., the Infrastructure Investment and Job Act of 2021 includes $47 billion investment in climate resilience and aims at helping communities build up resilience for the floods, storms, droughts, wildfires, and hurricanes.

Defining Climate Change Adaption and Resilience

There are no standard or agreed-upon definitions of climate change adaption and resilience. Below are a few examples of among variety of definitions of climate change adaptation:

- The Intergovernmental Panel on Climate Change (IPCC) defines adaption as "the process of adjustment to actual or expected climate and its effects. In human systems, adaptation seeks to moderate harm or exploit beneficial opportunities. In natural systems, human intervention may facilitate adjustment to expected climate and its effects...." (Noble et al., 2014).
- The U.S. Global Change Research Program (USGCRP)'s Fourth National Climate Assessment views adaptation as "actions taken at the individual, local, regional, and national levels to reduce risks from even today's changed climate conditions and to prepare for impacts from additional changes projected for the future."
- The U.S. Government Accountability Office (2013) has defined adaptation as "adjustments to natural or human systems in response to actual or expected climate change."

In sum, adaption generally means altering an existing system to accommodate persistent or long-term anticipated changes resulting from the climate change.

The following are a few examples of among variety of definitions of climate change resilience:

- Presidential Policy Directive 8 (2011) defines resilience as "the ability to adapt to changing conditions and withstand and rapidly recover from disruption due to emergencies."
- The United Nations International Strategy for Disaster Reduction (UNIDR) (2009) refers to resilience as "the ability of a system, community or society exposed to hazards to resist, absorb, accommodate to and recover from the

effects of a hazard in a timely and efficient manner, including through the preservation and restoration of its essential basic structures and functions" (p. 24).

- Willoughby et al. (2020) define resilience as "the ability of a locality to weather a natural disaster with the least losses in terms of human life, public and private property, and finances" (p. 6).

In sum, resilience generally means the capacity to anticipate, prepare for, withstand, absorb, accommodate to, and recover from disruptions due to emergencies and natural hazards.

What is a climate-resilient infrastructure system? According to Organization for Economic Co-operation and Development (OECD), the defining characteristic of a climate-resilient infrastructure system is that it is planned, designed, constructed, operated, and maintained in a way that anticipates, prepares for, and adapts to changing climate conditions (OECD, 2018, p. 4).[3] It is worthy to note that climate-resilient infrastructure differs from traditional infrastructure in two key aspects. On the one hand, it is less affected by the various impacts of climate changes. On the other hand, it facilitates the rapid recovery from future climate-exacerbated extreme events and ring sea levels (Meyer & Schwarze, 2019).

There are two types of climate-resilient infrastructure projects (O'Connell & Connors, 2019). One type is the gray infrastructure projects. They are traditionally engineered systems that provide benefits to water, drainage, or transportation systems through built structures such as seawalls, elevated roads, stormwater pipes, shoreline levees, pump stations, tidal gates, and wave attenuation devices. Another type is the green (or nature-based) infrastructure projects. They are based on ecological solutions and usually refer to natural or engineered infrastructure projects that mimic natural water cycles to manage stormwater and mitigate flood risk and extreme heat. The examples are open space preservation, wetland restoration, living shorelines, and green roofs. Green infrastructure projects provide an effective complement or substitute for traditional built (or gray) infrastructure. Table 2.1 illustrates the impacts of climate changes on electric power infrastructure and the resilience efforts for electric power infrastructure.

Sustainable investment should increase net wealth by turning financial capital (financial assets), human capital (human abilities), or natural capital

[3] There are varying definitions of climate-resilient infrastructure. For instance, Bhattacharya et al. (2016) define sustainable and resilient infrastructure as infrastructure that is built to adapt to the climate impacts and meet economic, environmental, and social goals. https://www.brookings.edu/research/delivering-on-sustainable-infrastructure-for-better-development-and-better-climate/.

Table 2.1 Example of electric power infrastructure resilience efforts

Electric power system	Climate impacts on electric power infrastructure	Resilience efforts for electric power infrastructure
Generation	Inundation of coastal infrastructure such as generation plants	Fortify coastal, off-shore, and flood-prone infrastructure against flooding
	Reduced efficiency of solar energy	Increase cooling system capacity for solar energy
	Insufficient cooling water	Locate new facilities outside high-risk zones
	Reduced output from hydropower generation	
Transmission and Distribution	Flooding of electricity substations	Adjust design criteria for transmission lines
	Damage to transmission lines from climate extreme	Bury distribution lines
		Use stainless steel material to reduce corrosion from water damage
Consumption	Change in energy demand patterns (e.g., increased demand for cooling and reduced demand for energy for heating)	Improve building and industrial energy efficiency

Source OECD (2018, p. 12)

(environmental assets) into physical capital (Leuenberger & Bartle, 2009). For example, an environmental construction project to reduce the pollution caused by stormwater runoff can increase community environmental assets (natural capital) by expending financial capital and physical capital. Not all sustainable investments put the environment first. For example, building a new highway can improve sustainability if the value of the transportation services delivered to users by the new highway is greater than the financial assets expended, and the diminution of environmental assets (air and water quality) caused by pollution. This focus on net community wealth provides a framework for evaluating the sustainability of capital planning decisions.

The CIP is a natural tool for state and local governments to develop a plan to improve community sustainability. State and local governments have the opportunity to incorporate sustainability and environmental resilience into the CIPs. Government officials and their citizens increasingly expect CIPs to align with state or community sustainability and resilience goals. The policy framework of CIPs can add environmental sustainability and climate resilience as criteria to prioritize and rank new infrastructure projects and require vulnerability assessment for proposed infrastructure projects. Furthermore, climate risk information needs to be updated regularly by government planning authorities to facilitate resilience planning efforts for infrastructure development. Done right, this is a way of operationalizing and implementing sustainability goals into the capital and financial plan of the government.

Integrating Resilience into Capital Planning in the City/County of San Francisco

San Francisco is surrounded on three sides by the Pacific Ocean and the San Francisco Bay. In recent years, the city has made a range of efforts in addressing key challenges that fact the city including earthquakes, climate change, sea level rise, and promoting infrastructure resilience:

- Created a new Office of Resilience and Capital Planning (within the San Francisco City Administrator' Office) to plan and finance projects that strengthen the integrity and resilience of San Francisco's infrastructure, neighborhoods, and residents,
- Adopted a capital planning document and incorporated climate risk into the city's capital planning process: *Guidance for Incorporating Sea Level Rise into Capital Planning in San Francisco: Assessing Vulnerability and Risk to Support Adaptation,*
- Created a disaster housing and governance capital plan for long-term recovery,
- Launched a regional resilience design challenge,
- Made the goal of constructing a disaster-resilient waterfront by 2040,
- Seismic retrofit of vulnerable buildings and set higher safety standards for new buildings,
- Promoted citywide adaptation planning for sea level rise.

Source The City and County of San Francisco. (2016). *Resilient San Francisco—Stronger Today, Stronger Tomorrow.* https://sfgsa.org/sites/default/files/Document/Resilient%20San%20Francisco.pdf.

2.6.2 Emerging Technologies

Emerging technological innovations have the potential of transforming infrastructure to meet new demands. For instance, nationally and globally, cities are embarking on efforts to harness the benefits of rapidly emerging technologies to improve quality of life, increase operational efficiency, enhance economic vitality, and improve sustainability. The concept of smart cities/states requires installing digital interfaces or smart technologies such as artificial intelligence, the Internet of Things, and blockchain in traditional infrastructure and creating smart city infrastructure systems. Smart infrastructure systems hold the promise of greater safety, higher energy efficiency, lower levels of pollution, and data-driven decision-making to improve capital services for citizens and businesses.

Connected and/or Autonomous Vehicle (CV/AV/CAV) technologies are among the most attractive automotive technologies, and they continue to evolve and rapidly develop new capabilities. The U.S. Department of Transportation's National Highway Traffic Safety Administration defines these vehicles as "those in which operation of the vehicle occurs without direct driver input to control the steering, acceleration, and braking and are designed so that the driver is not expected to constantly monitor the roadway while operating in self-driving mode" (US DOT, 2019). CV/AV/CAV have great potential not only to improve vehicle safety, but also to improve traffic mobility, efficiency, and sustainability (Maryland DOT, 2017). Government regulators have responded with a roadmap for autonomous vehicles and evolving guidance for developing the infrastructure to support them. The technologies that will require the most infrastructure changes are traffic sign recognition, automated assistance in roadwork and congestion, auto-valet parking, and driverless cars.

An electric vehicle (EV) is a vehicle that uses one or more electric motors or traction motors for propulsion (Diaz, 2020). EVs are gaining increased attention due to technological developments, an increased focus on renewable energy, and the potential reduction of transportation's impact on climate change and other environmental issues. With their potential for increasing energy security, economic vitality, and quality of life, plug-in EVs (including plug-in hybrid electric and all-electric) will likely play a vital role in the country's transportation future. As of 2020, about 1.8 million EVs were registered in the U.S., more than three times as many as in 2016 (Pew Research Center, 2021). Figure 2.4 shows the growth of EV sales in the U.S. from 2011 to 2020.

Given the growing popularity of EVs, state and local governments need to plan and expand electric vehicle charging infrastructure. Figure 2.5 shows the growth of U.S. public and private electric vehicle (EV) charging infrastructure since 2011. The number of electric vehicle supply equipment (EVSE) ports has grown consistently from 5,070 in 2011 to 106,814 in 2020, and the number of EV charging station locations has also increased steadily from 2,100 in 2011 to 31,738 in 2020. The bipartisan Infrastructure Investment and Jobs Act of 2021 provides $7.5 billion to jump start President Biden's goal of building a national network of 500,000 eV chargers by 2030. This represents the first-ever U.S. investment in electric vehicle charging stations.

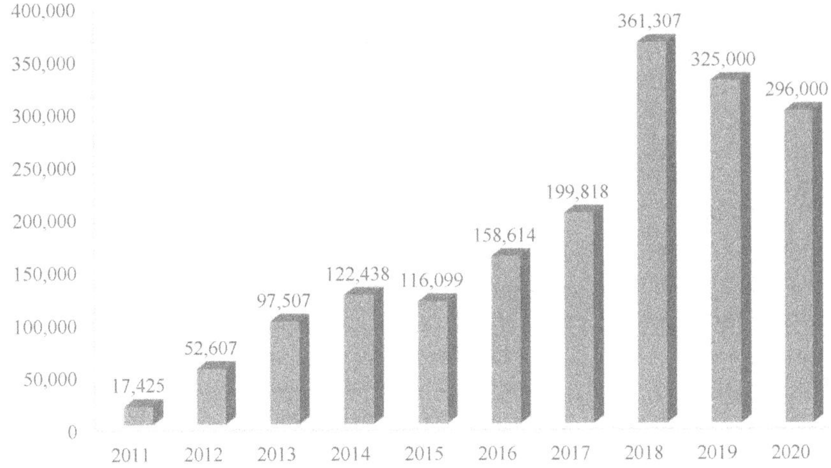

Fig. 2.4 U.S. electric vehicles sales: 2011–2020 (*Data source* https://evadoption.com/category/ev-sales-marketshare/)

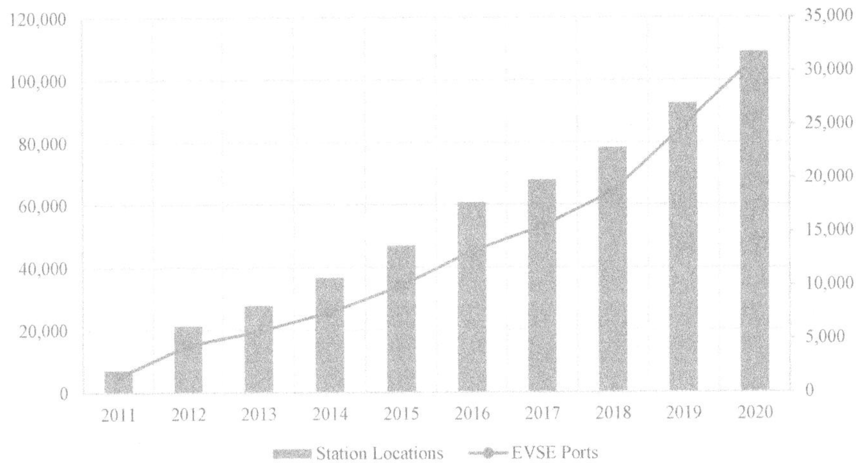

Fig. 2.5 U.S. public and private electric vehicle charging infrastructure (*Data source* U.S. Department of Energy: Alternative Fuels Data Center [afdc.energy.gov/stations/states])

Emerging technologies require adaptation of existing infrastructure and development of new infrastructure. Several ways are suggested to cope with these challenges and opportunities. First, state and local governments can highlight the concept of "smartness" during the capital planning stage and incorporated smartness and green principles into the priorities of ranking capital projects. Second, smart infrastructure systems usually involve multiple types of physical infrastructure, social infrastructure, and digital infrastructure. Planners and policymakers need to plan smart technologies and infrastructure on a holistic level and seek collaboration between public and private sectors. Third, the implementation of smart technologies requires more than installation. Careful capital planning related to infrastructure adaptability is needed for new technological development.

Fourth, due to the complexity of integrating systems and adopting emerging technologies, becoming a smarter city, county or state will take longer than a single budget cycle. It must be done in a phased approach that allows for planning major projects while building in enough flexibility to take advantage of the opportunities that arise and adjust tactics based on rapid changes. Fifth, state and local governments need to gain trust and support from the community to develop smart infrastructure. Public officials need to seek citizen input to gain buy-in and trust in capital planning and smart infrastructure project development. Sixth, financing smart infrastructure needs to use a wide variety of financial tools to secure capital funds for improvements. Capital improvements include upgrading existing infrastructure as well as implementing new smart digital infrastructure. Capital financing for smart infrastructure and new technologies can take advantage of grant opportunities, public–private partnerships, and other funding opportunities discussed in Chapter 4.

2.6.3 Integrating Racial and Gender Equity in Capital Planning

Racial inequality continues to be a challenging issue in education, employment, income, health, housing, poverty, and other social and economic areas which affect capital planning. In all these areas, African Americans and other minorities lag Whites. This is an issue for these minority groups and the overall health of American democracy and social equity. According to the U.S. Census Bureau, 39.7% of the population was estimated to be racial or ethnic minorities in 2019. The U.S. is projected to become "minority majority" nationwide in 2045: a plurality White (49.7%) in contrast to majority nonwhite (50.3%): 24.6% for Hispanics, 13.1% for Blacks, 7.9% for Asians, 3.8% for multiracial populations, and 0.9% for others (Frey, 2018).

Gender equity is also important in capital planning. While gender issues may not be immediately apparent, women tend to access some infrastructure in different ways than men. For example, transit is often focused on commuting to and from work; however, some women travel different directions at different times and carry infants or have them in a stroller. If the design and timing of subways and buses do not recognize these needs, then women do not receive the same level of service from transit infrastructure. Similarly, parks may not be designed in ways for women to feel safe, so women may not use parks early in the morning or later in the evening. Women's health needs are different than men's, so hospitals and healthcare facilities also need to accommodate these needs.

Racial, ethnic, and gender disparities are significant factors when examining infrastructure development. There has been increasing attention to racial inequalities in the development of infrastructure projects. Infrastructure projects were developed in a manner that often decimated Black neighborhoods. These disparities continue; communities of color have less access to high-speed Internet. The lead-contaminated water crisis in the majority Black city of Flint, Michigan, was mainly caused by structural and systemic discrimination and racism (Almasy & Ly, 2017). Black communities in particular face greater danger from the location of hazardous waste disposal facilities. Therefore, addressing racial inequities is an urgent and critical issue for state and local infrastructure planning and development. On his first day in office, President Biden issued Executive Order 13985, which called for the federal government to, among other things, "allocate resources to address the historic failure to invest sufficiently, justly, and equally in underserved communities, as well as individuals from those communities" (Biden, 2021). President Biden's 2021 American Jobs Plan includes $20 billion for the Reconnecting Communities Pilot Program which proposed re-engineering roads that adversely affected communities of color to address inequities and create opportunities for underserved neighborhoods. The Infrastructure Investment and Jobs Act of 2021 reduced this to $1 billion (Lobosco & Luhby, 2021), but advocates see this as a pilot program with potential.

In the face of continuing racial and gender disparities, there are several ways in which infrastructure planners and developers can spur positive change. First, infrastructure plays a critical role in equitable access to key systems that drive economic performance. To realize a more equitable and prosperous future, infrastructure should be planned and financed with the explicit goal of eliminating racial, ethnic, and gender disparities. Second, state and local governments need to more deliberately plan to address racial and gender inequities in infrastructure investment and prioritize infrastructure projects serving historically disinvested community areas and improving access for women. Stakeholders may realize better long-term returns by investing in projects that address existing gaps in racial and gender outcomes because they will be less likely to be affected by future regulatory changes. Third, state and local governments need to develop equity-based criteria for project selection and approval to determine whether we are investing in infrastructure equitably.

References

Almasy, S., & Ly, L. (2017). Flint water crisis: Report says 'systemic racism' played role. *CNN Politics*. https://www.cnn.com/2017/02/18/politics/flint-water-report-systemic-racism/index.html. Accessed on August 5, 2021.

Bhattacharya, A., Meltzer, J. P., Oppenheim, J., Qureshi, Z., & Stern, N. (2016). *Delivering on sustainable infrastructure for better development and better climate*. https://www.brookings.edu/research/delivering-on-sustainable-infrastructure-for-better-development-and-better-climate/. Accessed on August 5, 2021.

Birch, E., & Rodas, M. (2020). *The city climate-resilient infrastructure financing initiative*. https://penniur.upenn.edu/uploads/media/C2IFI_Brief.pdf. Accessed on November 23, 2021.

Biden, J. R., Jr. (2021). *Executive order on advancing racial equity and support for underserved communities through the federal government*. The White House: Executive Order 13985, 86 FR 7009–7013. Document Number: 2021-01753. https://www.whitehouse.gov/briefing-room/presidential-actions/2021/01/20/executive-order-advancing-racial-equity-and-support-for-underserved-communities-through-the-federal-government/. Accessed January 20, 2022.

Bunch, B. S. (2012). Capital planning and budgeting. In J. R. Bartle, W. B. Hildreth, & J. Marlowe (Eds.), *Management policies in local government finance* (pp. 253–278). International City/County Management Association Press.

City and County of San Francisco. (2016). *Resilient San Francisco—Stronger today, stronger tomorrow*. https://sfgsa.org/sites/default/files/Document/Resilient%20San%20Francisco.pdf. Accessed on September 22, 2021.

City of Miami. (2021). *FY 2022 proposed capital budget*. http://archive.miamigov.com/Budget/. Accessed on September 22, 2021.

County of Arlington. (2018). *Six-step public engagement guide for capital projects.* https://arlingtonva.s3.dualstack.us-east-1.amazonaws.com/wp-content/uploads/sites/21/2018/03/Six-Step-Public-Engagement-Guide-for-Capital-Projects.pdf. Accessed on September 22, 2021.

Diaz, M. N. (2020). *Electric vehicles: A primer on technology and selected policy issues.* https://crsreports.congress.gov/product/pdf/R/R46231. Accessed on August 5, 2021.

Frey, W. H. (2018). *The US will become 'minority white' in 2045, Census projects*. https://www.brookings.edu/blog/the-avenue/2018/03/14/the-us-will-become-minority-white-in-2045-census-projects/. Accessed on August 5, 2021.

Governmental Accounting Standards Board (GASB). (1999). *Statement No. 34, Basic Financial Statements—And Management's Discussion and Analysis—For State and Local Governments*. Norwalk, CT: GASB.

Governmental Accounting Standards Board (GASB). (2009). *Statement No. 51: Accounting for intangible assets*. https://www.gasb.org/st/summary/gstsm51.html. Accessed on September 22, 2021.

Intergovernmental Panel on Climate Change (IPCC). (2021). *The sixth assessment report*. https://www.ipcc.ch/assessment-report/ar6/. Accessed on November 23, 2021.

Lee, R. D., Jr, Johnson, R. W., & Joyce, P. G. (2021). *Public budgeting systems*. Jones & Bartlett Learning.

Leuenberger, D. Z., & Bartle, J. R. (2009). *Sustainable development for public administration*. M.E. Sharpe.

Lobosco, K., & Luhby, T. (2021). Here's what's in the bipartisan infrastructure bill. *CNN*, November 5. https://www.cnn.com/2021/07/28/politics/infrastructure-bill-explained/index.html. Accessed on November 8, 2021.

Marlowe, J., Rivenbark, W. C., & Vogt, A. J. (2009). *Capital budgeting and finance: A guide for local governments*. International City/County Management Association Press.

Maryland Department of Transportation. (2017). *Connected & automated vehicle (CAV) strategic action plan*. https://www.roads.maryland.gov/OTMO/MDOT%20SHA%20CAV%20Strategic%20Action%20Plan%20-%20FINAL%20-%20Dec%202017.pdf. Accessed on August 5, 2021.

Meyer, P. B., & Schwarze, R. (2019). *Financing climate-resilient infrastructure: A political-economy framework*. https://www.ufz.de/export/data/global/221987_DP_2019_1_Meyer-Schwarze.pdf. Accessed on November 23, 2021.

Mikesell, J. (2014). *Fiscal administration*. Cengage Learning.

National Association of State Budget Officers (NASBO). (2014). *Capital budget process in the State*. https://www.nasbo.org/mainsite/reports-data/capital-budgeting-in-the-states. Accessed on September 22, 2021.

National Oceanic and Atmospheric Administration. (2021). *2020 U.S. billion-dollar weather and climate disasters in historical context*. https://www.climate.gov/news-features/blogs/beyond-data/2020-us-billion-dollar-weather-and-climate-disasters-historical. Accessed on November 23, 2021.

Noble, I. R., Huq, S., Anokhin, Y. A., Carmin, J., et al. (2014). Adaptation needs and options. *IPCC*. https://www.ipcc.ch/site/assets/uploads/2018/02/WGIIAR5-Chap14_FINAL.pdf. Accessed on November 23, 2021.

O'Connell, L., & Connors, K. (2019). *Financing climate resilience: Funding and financing models for building green and resilient infrastructure in Florida*. https://www.hks.harvard.edu/sites/default/files/centers/research-initiatives/crisisleadership/files/financing_climate_resilience_final_report.pdf. Accessed on November 23, 2021.

OECD. (2018). *Climate-resilient infrastructure*. https://www.oecd.org/environment/cc/policy-perspectives-climate-resilient-infrastructure.pdf. Accessed on November 23, 2021.

Office of the New York State Comptroller. (2009). *Multiyear capital planning*. https://www.osc.state.ny.us/files/local-government/publications/pdf/capital_planning.pdf. Accessed on August 5, 2021.

Pew Research Center. (2021). *Today's electric vehicle market: Slow growth in U.S., faster in China, Europe*. https://www.pewresearch.org/fact-tank/2021/06/07/todays-electric-vehicle-market-slow-growth-in-u-s-faster-in-china-europe/. Accessed on August 5, 2021.

Presidential Policy Directive 8. (2011). *National Preparedness (PPD-8)*. https://www.fema.gov/emergency-managers/national-preparedness. Accessed on November 23, 2021.

The City and County of San Francisco. (2016). *Resilient San Francisco—Stronger today, stronger tomorrow*. https://sfgsa.org/sites/default/files/Document/Resilient%20San%20Francisco.pdf. Accessed on December 7, 2021.

The County of Arlington, Virginia. (2018). *Six-step public engagement guide for capital projects*. https://arlingtonva.s3.dualstack.us-east-1.amazonaws.com/wp-content/uploads/sites/21/2018/03/Six-Step-Public-Engagement-Guide-for-Capital-Projects.pdf. Accessed on December 7, 2021.

The Global Commission on Adaptation. (2019). *Adapt now: A global call for leadership on climate resilience*. https://gca.org/wp-content/uploads/2019/09/GlobalCommission_Report_FINAL.pdf. Accessed on November 23, 2021.

The United Nations International Strategy for Disaster Reduction (UNIDR). (2009). *UNISDR terminology on disaster risk reduction*. https://www.unisdr.org/files/7817_UNISDRTerminologyEnglish.pdf. Accessed on November 23, 2021.

The United Nations Environment Programme (UNEP). (2016). *The adaptation finance gap report*. https://climateanalytics.org/media/agr2016.pdf. Accessed on November 23, 2021.

United Nation. (1992). *The United Nations framework convention on climate change*. https://unfccc.int/files/essential_background/background_publications_htmlpdf/application/pdf/conveng.pdf. Accessed on November 23, 2021.

United States President's Commission to Study Capital Budgeting. (1999). *Report of the President's commission to study capital budgeting*. https://clintonwhitehouse3.archives.gov/pcscb/report.html. Accessed on August 5, 2021.

U.S. Census Bureau. (2019). 94.*7 M American live in Coastline Regions*. https://www.census.gov/library/stories/2019/07/millions-of-americans-live-coastline-regions.html. Accessed on August 5, 2021.

U.S. Department of Energy. (2021). *Electric vehicle charging station locations*. https://afdc.energy.gov/fuels/electricity_locations.html#/find/nearest?fuel=ELEC&country=US&ev_levels=all. Accessed on August 5, 2021.

U.S. Department of Transportation. (2019). U.S. Department of Transportation releases Policy on Automated Vehicle Development. https://www.transportation.

gov/briefing-room/us-department-transportation-releases-policy-automated-vehicle-development. Accessed on August 5, 2021.

U.S. Government Accountability Office (GAO). (1987). *Capital budgeting for the federal government*. https://www.gao.gov/products/t-afmd-88-3. Accessed on August 5, 2021.

U.S. Government Accountability Office. (2013). *Climate change: Future federal adaptation efforts could better support local infrastructure decision makers*. https://www.gao.gov/assets/gao-13-242.pdf. Accessed on November 23, 2021.

U.S. Global Change Research Program. (2018). *Impacts, risks, and adaptation in the United States: Fourth National Climate Assessment*. https://nca2018.globalchange.gov/downloads/NCA4_2018_FullReport.pdf. Accessed on November 23, 2021.

U.S. National Oceanic and Atmospheric Administration (NOAA). (2021). *Fact facts of hurricane costs*. https://coast.noaa.gov/states/fast-facts/hurricane-costs.html. Accessed on August 5, 2021.

White House. (2021). *Fact sheet: The American job plan*. https://www.whitehouse.gov/briefing-room/statements-releases/2021/03/31/fact-sheet-the-american-jobs-plan/. Accessed August 3, 2021.

Willoughby, K., Dzigbede, K.D., & Gehl, S. B. (2020). *How localities continually adapt enterprise strategies to manage natural disasters*. IBM Center for the Business of Government. https://www.businessofgovernment.org/report/how-localities-continually-adapt-enterprise-strategies-manage-natural-disasters. Accessed on November 23, 2021.

3

Traditional Methods of Financing Infrastructure

This chapter focuses on the traditional ways of financing infrastructure. The first section elaborates the main rationales of public provision of infrastructure and highlights the key differences between infrastructure "funding" and "financing." The second section briefly depicts the two methods of financing infrastructure: pay-as-you-go and pay-as-you-use. The third section discusses the strengths and weaknesses of a wide variety of traditional infrastructure funding sources and financing methods.

3.1 Fundamentals of Infrastructure Finance

3.1.1 Why Do Governments Provide Infrastructure?

As discussed in Chapter 1, market failure is the primary economic rationale for government provision of infrastructure. There are several forms of market failure in the private provision of infrastructure. The first form is public goods. Private goods have two defining characteristics: rivalry in consumption and excludability in ownership and use. Instead, public goods are, in varying degrees, non-rival in consumption, non-excludable in use, or both. The classic example of a pure public good is national defense. Infrastructure (e.g., street lighting) is traditionally viewed as public goods.[1] Because of the

[1] Nowadays, as technology advances, some types of infrastructure do not fall into the category of a pure public good. For example, an electronic toll road is clearly excludable.

C. Chen and J. R. Bartle, *Innovative Infrastructure Finance*,
https://doi.org/10.1007/978-3-030-91411-0_3

nature of public goods, private markets tend to undersupply infrastructure. Second, infrastructure often displays external benefits or positive externalities. For instance, it is generally recognized that ready access to highway infrastructure has positive externalities for shippers. In the presence of externalities, the private market does not provide an efficient output level and public intervention may be appropriate. Third, natural monopoly is another rationale for government involvement in infrastructure. A natural monopoly may exist due to the high fixed costs or powerful economies of scale, which can create significant barriers to entry for potential competitors. This may cause the monopolist to undersupply the goods and charge higher prices. Large urban infrastructure (such as public utilities) often constitutes natural monopolies.

In addition to market failure, governments often make substantive infrastructure investments to create more jobs and stimulate the economy during times of economic crisis. For example, the American Recovery and Reinvestment Act of 2009 (ARRA) was a massive fiscal policy adopted by the federal government to help stimulate the economy after the Great Recession of 2007–2009. The U.S. Congressional Budget Office (CBO) estimated that ARRA cost the federal government $787 billion from FY 2009 through FY 2019 (U.S. CBO, 2015). Infrastructure investment programs were a major part of ARRA. According to Mallett (2020), it was estimated that infrastructure investment accounted for approximately $100 billion to $150 billion (13% to 19% of total ARRA spending).

Transportation Infrastructure Investment as Economic Stimulus: The American Recovery and Reinvestment Act of 2009

- The "Great Recession" began in December 2008 and ended in June 2009. It was the most severe economic downturn since the Great Depression of the 1930s. The recession was relatively deep and the recovery relatively slow. The unemployment rate rose from 4.4% in May 2007 to 10% in October 2009.
- The American Recovery and Reinvestment Act of 2009 (ARRA) was a fiscal stimulus package that passed on February 17, 2009, with the purpose of responding to the "Great Recession." The CBO estimated that ARRA cost the federal government $787 billion from FY 2009 through FY 2019.
- The US Congress provided mass infrastructure funding for economic stimulus in ARRA. ARRA provided $48.1 billion for transportation infrastructure investment. It included $27.5 billion for highways, $8.4 billion for public transportation, $8.0 billion for high-speed rail, $1.3 billion for Amtrak, $1.3 billion for aviation programs, and $1.5 billion for Transportation Investment Generating Economic Recovery (TIGER) grants. ARRA transportation funding was distributed by US DOT agencies via existing formula programs

Source Mallett, W. J. (2020). *Transportation Infrastructure Investment as Economic Stimulus: Lessons from the American Recovery and Reinvestment Act of 2009*. US Congressional Research Service. https://fas.org/sgp/crs/misc/R46343.pdf.

On November 15, 2021, President Biden signed the Infrastructure Investment and Jobs Act which "will deliver $550 billion of new federal investments in America's infrastructure over five years, touching everything from bridges and roads to the nation's broadband, water and energy systems" (Lobosco & Luhby, 2021).

The U.S. Infrastructure Investment and Jobs Act of 2021: Breaking it Down

- The Infrastructure Investment and Jobs Act of 2021 (IIJA) was signed by President Biden on November 15, 2021. IIJA is a historic public infrastructure investment law that will make available $1.2 trillion in funding for infrastructure programs across the transportation, water, and energy sectors, through a combination of grants, loans, and tax incentives.
- Of the $1.2 trillion in infrastructure funding, $550 billion is new federal spending not previously authorized. It consists of $284 billion (roads, bridges, passenger and freight rail, airports, ports, waterways, public transit, electric vehicles, safety, and reconnecting communities) and $266 billion (the society's core infrastructure—the power grid, broadband, water, environmental resilience, and remediation). IIJA also reauthorizes the federal highway, public transportation, and rail programs for five years (Fig. 3.1).

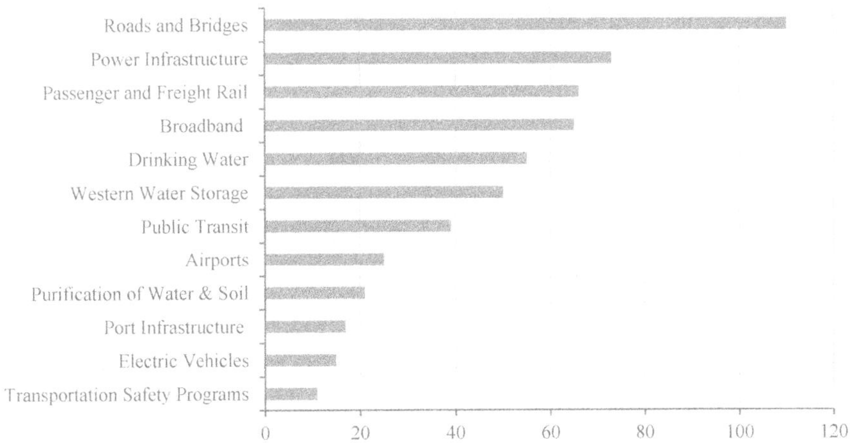

Fig. 3.1 U.S. infrastructure investment and jobs act: New $550 billon federal infrastructure funding (Unit: Billion Dollar) (*Data source* U.S. Congress (2021)

- The U.S. Department of Transportation (US DOT) will direct the largest portion of the IIJA's investment. Several other federal agencies will also see their budgets expand such as U.S. Environmental Protection Agencies, U.S. Department of Energy, U.S. Department of the Interior U.S. Department of Commerce, Department of Homeland Security, and others.

Source U.S. Congress. (2021). *H.R.3684—Infrastructure Investment and Jobs Act.* https://www.congress.gov/bill/117th-congress/house-bill/3684.

3.1.2 What Makes Infrastructure Finance Special?

Infrastructure projects have several key features that make their financing different than other government spending. First, spending tends to be large, up-front investments that require significant capital outlay. The second feature is the long economic life of most infrastructure assets. Third, infrastructure projects are often complex and involve a wide range of stakeholders—design and construction companies, operators, government authorities, financiers, private investors, insurers, and citizens. Fourth, large-scale infrastructure projects often benefit a wide range of people who are difficult to measure and be charged. In sum, due to the large capital outlay, the long-time horizon, complexity, and significant externalities; infrastructure projects often involve higher risks, making efficient and prudent financing of infrastructure critical. Mistakes in infrastructure development or financing can be a burden for many years for a community: the proverbial "white elephant."

3.1.3 What are the Differences Between Infrastructure Funding and Financing?

Infrastructure funding decisions are different from financing decisions. *Funding* refers to a revenue stream that pays for or offsets the cost of an infrastructure project or supports the repayment of debt that finances the infrastructure project. It may consist of revenue from local tax receipts or grants or the proceeds of debt financing. A large infrastructure project typically involves multiple funding sources, including federal, state, and local sources. *Financing* is not a source of revenue. It refers to the method of paying for infrastructure, including debt financing, typically through a bond, but also through loans or other debt mechanisms such as a line of credit. Similar to a home mortgage, the debt must be paid back over time with interest. A source of revenue must be secured to repay the debt, whether it is future federal and state grants, local taxes, or other sources. For example, a city government may borrow money (the financing) to pay the cost of building a new local street and repay that loan from a recurring tax (the funding). The tax or source of repayment is referred to as the security of the borrowing.

3.2 State and Local Infrastructure Financing: Pay-Go vs. Pay-Use

In general, state and local governments rely on two methods of financing infrastructure: pay-as-you-go (pay-go, or cash and savings) and pay-as-you-use (pay-use, or debt) (Marlowe et al., 2009). *Pay-go financing* refers to using cash or other current assets rather than borrowing money to pay for infrastructure projects. The key advantages of pay-go financing are that it is very simple and less expensive. Its key disadvantages are having to wait until sufficient funds have accumulated and placing an excessive burden on current taxpayers. Pay-go financing is most commonly used in cases when capital projects are small or have shorter useful lives, when capital reserves or set-aside funds are sufficient to fund an infrastructure project, when project sponsors have limited access to debt, when local governments are approaching their debt limits, or there are prohibitions on the use of debt.

Pay-use financing considers borrowing the funds needed (e.g., issuing long-term debt in the form of general obligation bonds or revenue bonds) to pay for infrastructure projects and then repaying those funds over time. Infrastructure projects often involve large or lumpy investments and benefit both current taxpayers and future generations. Using future revenues to fund these projects is justified because it achieves greater intergenerational equity. Debt financing is justified in part by spreading out the costs of public infrastructure investments throughout the life of the project and paying the bonds over the asset life. There are several disadvantages to pay-use financing. First, the process of debt financing is lengthy. It takes a relatively long time to issue the bonds. Second, the use of debt finance is complicated and involves multiple professionals such as financial advisors, underwriters, and lawyers, which may be expensive. Third, the use of debt financing is subject to legal limits and must comply with constitutional and statutory limits and restrictions, as well as tax laws and bond covenants. Pay-use financing is most used in cases when the infrastructure project has a long useful life, when the project is too expensive to be reasonably developed with currently available resources, and when borrowing rates compare favorably.

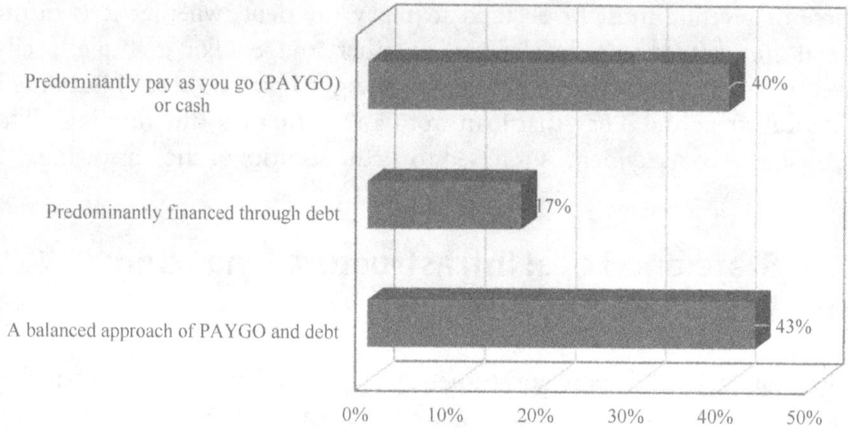

Fig. 3.2 Local infrastructure financing strategies (*Data source* ICMA [2017])

Pay-Go and Pay-Use Capital Financing

- In 2016, the International City/County Management Association (ICMA) surveyed roughly 5,500 governments on innovative financing, with 601 responding for a response rate of 11% (ICMA, 2017).
- The survey results provide information on the infrastructure financing strategies among US local governments: 43% of local government respondents use a balanced approach of Pay-Go and debt financing, 40% of respondents predominantly use a Pay-Go or cash approach. Only 17% of local government respondents relied heavily on infrastructure through debt financing (Fig. 3.2).
- Wang, Hou, and Duncombe (2007) analyzed the determinants of the use of pay-go financing (measured as the share of capital expenditures from the general fund) for state capital expenditures from 1988 to 2003. The authors found that the use of pay-go capital financing is affected by state economic conditions (income, credit rating) and political characteristics (the presence of divided governments) as well as state budgetary institutions (the requirement of a GO debt referendum, stringent balanced budget requirements, expenditure limits, and line-item veto).
- In a follow-up study, Wang and Hou (2009) explored the effect of pay-go capital financing on state government capital outlay volatility. They found that the use of pay-go capital financing is associated with lower volatility in capital spending in the long run but may increase short-run variability. The authors suggest that states couple pay-go capital financing in boom years with pay-use in lean years.

The infrastructure financing decision regarding the use of pay-go or pay-use depends on the following considerations:

- *When is the infrastructure project needed?* The urgency of capital needs is essential in deciding whether to use pay-go or pay-use. Suppose an infrastructure project is needed immediately because of legal or regulatory mandates or critical failure of existing infrastructure and governments' lack of adequate financial resources to build it. In that case, debt financing becomes the logical way to finance this project.
- *Are there enough funding sources on hand to pay for the project?* Governments need to carefully consider the affordability of using pay-go financing for infrastructure development projects. They should avoid situations where the operating budget would be under too much stress.
- *Do governments have access to the capital markets?* In capital markets, participants buy and sell short and long-term debt or equity-backed securities. In the U.S., state and local governments are important players in capital markets, both as issuers of debt securities to pay for infrastructure, and as investors who invest to manage their cash or meet employee retirement system needs. To use debt financing, a governmental jurisdiction should be able to access capital markets by maintaining a good credit rating and providing reasonable assurance to investors that debt obligation will be repaid as promised.
- *Is there available capacity for borrowing?* Government borrowing—particularly general obligation bonds—is generally constrained by legal debt limits or requirements. "How much debt can you afford?" is a very important question that should be answered when governmental jurisdictions consider the issuance of debt to finance infrastructure projects. Three primary factors influence debt capacity: expenditure pressures, resource availability, and voters' willingness to support new debt (Lee et al., 2021).
- *Are there concerns about intergenerational equity?* Intergenerational equity attempts to align the useful life of the infrastructure project with the period during which those benefiting from the infrastructure development are paying for it. Sharing the cost of infrastructure development with future generations improves intergenerational equity. If the project relies too heavily on current residents, debt financing is a good choice.

3.3 Traditional Infrastructure Financing Methods and Funding Sources

Whether the choice is pay-go or pay-use capital financing, sources for funding state and local infrastructure generally come from local general taxes, special funds such as dedicated user fees and earmarked taxes, intergovernmental grants, bond proceeds, or some combination of these sources.

For example, local sources for funding highways primarily include federal and state highway aid, general fund appropriations, tolls, taxes, and bond proceeds. Municipal wastewater and drinking water infrastructure projects have largely been funded by local wastewater and water supply user fee charges and private market debt, with the remainder of the funding from federal and state grants.

When considering the funding sources for an infrastructure project, governments need to decide how to share the project costs between the primary users of the project and other stakeholders such as general taxpayers. As illustrated in Fig. 3.3, the infrastructure improvements at the bottom of the pyramid offer broad benefits to a wide array of users, so it is appropriate to fund the infrastructure project from the general taxpayers. By contrast, the infrastructure improvements at the top of the pyramid are much narrower in their use, so it is suitable to have the primary users pay for the cost of infrastructure improvement. The other examples in the middle logically involve sharing the costs among primary and general users.

State and local governments have a variety of methods that provide traditional infrastructure financing, and each method has its unique strengths and weaknesses. Table 3.1 provides a list of these traditional financing methods and funding sources.

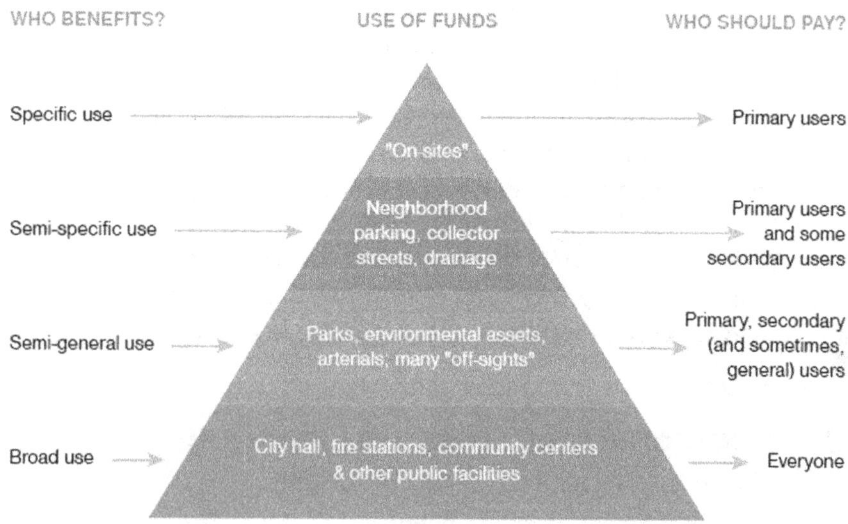

Fig. 3.3 Taxpayer equity (*Source* The California Debt and Investment Advisory Commission [2021])

Table 3.1 Traditional methods of state and local infrastructure financing

Pay-As-You-Go financing cash and savings	Pay-As-You-Use Financing debt financing
Taxation	Loan Financing
·General Taxes	·Private Bank Loans
·Special Dedicated Taxes	Bond Financing
Fees and user charges	·General Obligation Bonds
Capital reserves and fund balance	·Revenue Bonds
Federal grants and aid	·Private Activities Bonds
State grants and aid	·Leasing-Revenue Bonds

Source The Authors

3.3.1 Cash and Savings

General Taxes. Tax revenue is commonly used in state and local infrastructure financing. General taxes refer to broad-based taxes on residents and businesses. They consist of sales tax, property tax, and income or wage taxes. They are often used to finance infrastructure projects that yield community-wide benefits such as state and local highways, streets, transit, and parks and recreation. Using general tax revenues to finance infrastructure has the advantage of employing large tax bases and relatively stable and predictable tax revenues. However, some general taxes such as state and local option sales tax are regressive and may impose a larger burden on low-income people than higher-income people. In addition, in many cases, increases in these general taxes may be subject to voter approval. This approval process may face considerable public resistance and take longer, delaying the timely construction of needed infrastructure.

Special Dedicated Taxes. In addition to general taxes, many state and local governments use more narrowly based taxes either in their general funds or in special funds and dedicate these revenues to fund infrastructure projects. State and local option gas taxes, local utility taxes, telecommunication taxes, gaming taxes, and hotel and other occupancy taxes are often deposited into a special revenue fund. Some or all these revenues can be earmarked for infrastructure purposes. The key advantage of earmarking special tax revenues is that this protects infrastructure spending from competition from other uses of these funds. Furthermore, some taxes, such as local hotel/motel taxes, largely charge non-residents for using local infrastructure. However, disadvantages include volatility of special revenue sources, such as gaming and tourism taxes, and earmarking financing, which may restrict the flexibility and discretion of government officials in the fiscal planning process.

Transportation Trust Funds

- In the U.S., the federal government historically has used motor fuel taxes to pay for transportation investments in highways and transit systems.
- The Highway Trust Fund finances most federal government spending for highways and mass transit. Revenues for the trust fund come from transportation-related excise taxes, primarily federal taxes on gasoline and diesel fuel (a federal fuel tax of 18.4 cents per gallon on gasoline and 24.4 cents per gallon of diesel fuel and related excise taxes). In recent years, however, the trust fund has needed significant transfers of general revenues to remain solvent.
- All states levy motor fuel taxes. Nineteen states earmark state motor fuel taxes into a state transportation trust fund. Some other states use a designated account for such receipts. The use of state transportation funds or accounts is proscribed by constitutional or statutory provision in at least 35 states. The use of state fuel tax revenues exclusively for highway and road purposes has been imposed constitutionally in 23 states and statutorily in 3 others. Some states, such as New York, Massachusetts, and New Jersey divert significant portions of state motor fuel tax revenues to fund transit systems (Bartle & Chen, 2015).

Fees and User Charges. User charges play a crucial role in local infrastructure finance, particularly for toll roads, parking facilities, drinking water, wastewater, and solid waste disposal. Fees are also imposed on residents and businesses for their use of utilities and other public enterprises, including tolls, motor vehicle license and registration fees, congestion pricing, transit fares, airport terminal use fees, water charges, sewer charges, franchise fees, parking fees, and others.

User charges are typically collected into an enterprise fund that accounts for state and local government business-type activities. Infrastructure projects such as water, wastewater, parking facilities, and convention centers are often funded by user charges through an enterprise fund. Significant user charges such as water utility fees can be used as the dedicated revenue source to secure revenue bonds. User-charge financing is advantageous because it functions to recover partial or full costs of the consumed government services and to offer price signals and incentives to influence consumers' choices (Anderson, 2012; Fisher, 2007). It may be politically easier to use user charges to fund revenue-generating infrastructure projects than to use general taxes. The downsides of relying on user charges are their regressive nature and the high cost of collection.

Capital Reserves and Fund Balance. State and local governments regularly save and accumulate money in capital reserve funds and then designate the funds to pay for recurring and small capital projects (Bunch, 2012; Marlowe et al., 2009). Capital reserves have the advantage of reducing debt issuance and preserving flexibility in future operating budgets. However, saving sufficient money takes time. During tough fiscal periods, capital reserve funds may be diverted to support operations. Moreover, the use of capital reserves is confined to less expensive capital projects.

Four Percent Capital Reserve Fund in the Metropolitan Government of Nashville and Davidson County, Tennessee

- ***Overview:*** The Metropolitan Government of Nashville and Davidson County (Metro) creates a Four Percent Capital Reserve Fund to finance small-to-medium size capital expenditures for General Services District (GSD) General Fund departments.
- ***Revenues:*** Four percent of all revenues collected by the GSD General Fund are deposited into this capital reserve fund except for revenues from other governments and other internal sources and transfer accounts.
- ***Expenditures:*** This fund can only be spent for repairing buildings and purchasing new equipment for the Metro departments. Larger capital expenditures are inappropriate for using this capital reserve fund.
- ***Minimum Balance:*** A minimum of $500,000 balance needs to be maintained in the fund. The Council recently raised the limit of minimum balance. Now, the capital reserve fund needs to maintain at least $ 1 million for the minimum fund balance.

Source Metropolitan Government of Nashville and Davidson County. (2020). *30003 4% Reserve Fund—At a Glance*. https://filetransfer.nashville.gov/portals/0/sitecontent/Finance/docs/OMB/fy21_budget/Recommended/30003-4PercentReserveFund.pdf.

In addition to capital reserve funds, state and local governments can set up a capital asset replacement fund (sinking fund) to pay for the future replacement of government buildings, equipment, facilities, vehicles, and certain other assets. A capital asset replacement fund is operated as an internal service fund that charges government departments and agencies a service fee for the use of equipment, facilities, and vehicles (Marlowe et al., 2009). Like a capital reserve fund, a capital asset replacement fund may not be reliable during tough fiscal times because it may be diverted into the general fund for operations. Under certain circumstances, general fund balances become a source for infrastructure financing. When state and local governments' general undesignated fund balance reaches a certain threshold, any additional funds (or a specific portion of them) may be used to purchase major equipment or to help fund infrastructure projects (Bunch, 2012).

Intergovernmental Grants and Aid. Federal grants represent a major funding source of state and local infrastructure financing. State grant funds also aid local governments. A variety of federal grant programs is available to help fund local infrastructure. For example, the Fixing America's Surface Transportation Act (FAST Act) was signed into law on December 4, 2015. The FAST Act extended federal highway and transit funding from the fiscal year 2016 to 2020 and offered a total funding amount of $305 billion to help improve state and local transportation-related development activities and expand transportation modes (see Table 3.2).

Popular federal transportation grant programs include surface transportation block grant programs, grants for buses and bus facilities, and fixed guideway capital improvement grants. The EPA provides capitalization grants for state clean water and drinking water revolving funds, which provide low-cost loans to local communities to finance drinking water and wastewater infrastructure improvements.

Since 1974, the U.S. Department of Housing and Urban Development (HUD) has administered the Community Development Block Grant (CDBG) program, which can be used for community development projects such as water and wastewater improvements, community/public facilities, public housing, and smaller public works projects. It should be noted that federal infrastructure grants have been less stable and predictable in recent years, which makes it harder for states and localities to do long-term capital planning. For instance, the Federal Highway Trust Fund continues to face insolvency because lawmakers have failed to achieve consensus on a long-term funding solution. In addition, federal infrastructure-related program spending, including CDBG and EPA funding, is declining.

Besides federal grants, state-funded grants and aid programs are available in many states to help fund local streets, bridges, water supply and wastewater utilities, parks and recreation, facilities and equipment for law enforcement, and many other local infrastructure needs. Many state governments provide simpler grants to help smaller and rural communities improve local water and sewer infrastructure.

Federal and state grants have the advantages of sharing the cost of infrastructure projects and enabling local governments to fund needed capital projects. However, federal and state governments have their own policy goals and priorities in designing grant programs. External grantors have different priorities than local jurisdictions. Additionally, federal and state governments often impose hard restrictions on the local government recipients' use of intergovernmental grants. Finally, most federal and state grants target local capital construction rather than maintenance, which may increase the burden on local governments to maintain infrastructure.

Table 3.2 History of federal transportation aid to state and local governments

Year	Federal aid structure and uses
Early 1900s	Federal highway aid begins
1921	Federal aid restricted to principal roads connecting states or counties within states
1944	Rural secondary roads and principal urban highways added to federal aid system by Federal Highway Aid Act. Matching grants used with 75% federal and 25% state-local shares. Federal aid road system includes rural primary roads, rural secondary roads, and urban extensions of rural primary roads
1954	Urban extensions of rural secondary roads added to federal aid system
1956	Substantial grants for Interstate and Defense Highway System begun with 90% federal and 10% state shares. Highway Trust Fund created by the Highway Revenue Act to receive transportation related taxes and charges
1964	Grants for mass transit capital costs instituted, to cover up to two-thirds of the cost
1970	Separate grants for bridge rehabilitation and replacement instituted
1973	Maximum federal grant share for mass transit capital costs increased to 80%, still the current rate
1974	Grants for mass transit operating costs at a 50/50 share instituted
1976	Specific grants for resurfacing, restoration, and rehabilitation of interstate highways provided
1983	Surface Transportation Assistance Act increased federal gasoline tax from $0.04 to $0.09 per gallon with $0.04 of the increase restricted to aid for interstate and rural primary roads only and $0.01 earmarked for mass transit capital grants
1991	Intermodal Surface Transportation Efficiency Act (ISTEA) revamped the federal aid system, creating a new National Highway System to include Interstate highways, most urban and rural principal arterials, and strategic connectors. The Interstate System is to be completed by 1995, with continuing funds for Interstate resurfacing and rehabilitation at a 90% federal share. The Surface Transportation Program provides grants for local or rural roads, bridges, and mass transit capital projects
1993	Federal gasoline tax increased to $0.184 with $0.10 for highway aid, $0.015 earmarked for mass transit capital grants, and $0.068 for deficit reduction. In October 1995, the division changes to $0.12 for highways, $0.02 for mass transit, and $0.043 for deficit reduction

(continued)

Table 3.2 (continued)

Year	Federal aid structure and uses
1998	Transportation Equity Act for the twenty-first century (TEA-21) extended most transportation user taxes and allocations through September 30, 2005. Federal aid for highways was increased and allocation formulas changed to direct more revenue to growing states, essentially those in the Sun Belt. The transit share of the gasoline tax was increased to $0.0286
2005	Safe, Accountable, Flexible, and Efficient Transportation Equity Act: A Legacy for Users (SAFETEA-LU) adopted just before provisions of TEA-21 were to expire. It extends highway-user taxes at current rates through September 30, 2011. States will be guaranteed a minimum 92 % return on contributions to the Highway trust Fund. States receive increased flexibility to use tolls and other forms of road pricing to manage congestion and to finance infrastructure improvements
2012	Moving Ahead for Progress in the twenty-first Century Act (MAP-21) funded surface transportation programs at over $105 billion for fiscal years 2013 and 2014. MAP-21 expands the National Highway System to incorporate principal arterials not previously included. MAP-21 authorized $82 billion for road, bridge, bicycling, and walking improvements as well as doubled funding for infrastructure safety
2015	The Fixing America's Surface Transportation Act (FAST) funded surface transportation programs at $305 billion for fiscal years 2016 and 2020. The FAST provided $225.2 billion in Highway Trust Fund (HTF), including $10.7 billion for two highway freight initiatives: the National Highway Freight Program and the new Nationally Significant Freight and Highway Projects program, also known as FASTLANE grants. The FAST Signals a renewed emphasis on improving safety on our nation's highways, and it gives state and local governments' assurance that they have federal funding for long-term critical surface and rail transportation-safety projects

Source Fisher (2016, pp. 543–544), U.S. Department of Transportation (2015). https://www.transportation.gov/fastact

3.3.2 Debt Financing

Debt financing is the most common type of long-term borrowing that states and localities use to fund the building and construction of long-lived infrastructure assets. In the U.S., the municipal bond market plays a crucial role in state and local capital financing. In 2019, state and local governments invested nearly $409 billion in capital projects (U.S. Census Bureau, 2021). Most state and local capital spending is financed by debt. As discussed above, the lumpiness of infrastructure projects and intergenerational equity justify debt funding. Spreading out the costs of public infrastructure investments over several years may be beneficial. In addition, state and local governments can quickly obtain needed capital and build capital projects without significant delay.

Private Bank Loans. Typically, state and local government debt takes the form of either a private bank loan (loan financing) or a municipal bond (bond financing). State and local governments can secure direct loans from private commercial banks, industrial loan companies, or industrial banks. It is estimated that bank financing of public infrastructure projects has grown to over $155 billion, with another $25 to $30 billion being added each year (Kelly, 2016). Using bank loans is advantageous, especially for small governments with limited access to the municipal bond market and cannot afford the costs of bond issuance. However, compared to municipal bonds, private loan financing is usually more expensive and less transparent and does not disclose information to investors to the same degree (Kelly, 2016).

Bond Financing. Instead of securing loans from private banks, state and local governments frequently choose to issue bonds to municipal capital investors (bond buyers) to raise the needed capital to finance the construction of new capital projects or refinance existing bonds. The borrower is then obligated to repay debt service (bond principal and interest payments). Because interest income from publicly issued bonds is generally exempt from federal and some state income taxes, state and local governments can obtain lower interest rates than corporate bonds, which significantly reduces the costs of issuing bonds. According to a report sponsored by ICMA and the Government Finance Officers Association (GFOA), state and local governments would have paid $714 billion in additional interest expenses from 2000 to 2014 if the federal tax exemption for municipal bonds were repealed (Marlowe, 2015).

The Municipal Bond Market in the U.S.

- The term "municipal bonds" or "munis" refer to debt securities issued by states, counties, cities, school districts, public utilities, ports, and other sub-national government-created agencies to finance capital projects such as bridges, highways, airports, sewers, and others (U.S. Congressional Research Service, 2015). According to the Securities Industry and Financial Markets Association (SIFMA), the U.S. municipal bond market has $4.0 trillion of debt outstanding at the end of the second quarter of 2021 (SIFMA, 2021).
- Since the creation of federal income tax in 1913, interest payments on government purpose municipal bonds have been exempt from federal

income tax (tax-exempt municipal bonds). State and local governments also typically exempt interest on bonds issued by taxpayers' state of residence.

- In the U.S., state and local governments can choose different methods of sale: competitive bidding, negotiation, or private placement (Lee et al., 2021)
  - In a competitive bid, the bonds are advertised for public sale and awarded to the lowest bidder.
  - In a negotiated sale, an underwriter (a large investment bank) is chosen to purchase the bonds. Once the underwriter is selected, the issuing government then work with the underwriter to develop a bond issue. The underwriter functions as a broker between the issuing government and the investment community.
  - Private placement bonds are unregistered debt securities that are sold to accredited investors via investment banks.
- Municipal bonds may be new issuances or refunding issuances. Like refinancing a housing mortgage, state and local governments can "refund" or "retire" existing tax-exempt municipal bonds by issuing new bonds to pay off the existing ones, typically at a lower interest rate or at more favorable terms. This refunding will yield borrowing cost saving over time.

Source U.S. Congressional Research Service. (2015). *The demand for municipal bonds: Issues for congress.* https://crsreports.congress.gov/product/pdf/R/R44146. The Securities Industry and Financial Markets Association (SIFMA). (2021). *US-Municipal-Bonds-Statistics-SIFMA.* https://www.sifma.org/resources/research/us-municipal-bonds-statistics/us-municipal-bonds-statistics-sifma/. Lee Jr, R. D., Johnson, R. W., & Joyce, P. G. (2021). *Public budgeting systems.* Jones & Bartlett Learning.

In 1950, the number of state and local governments debt outstanding was $0.02 trillion. In the end of 2020, state and local governments had $3.2 trillion in outstanding debt (Fig. 3.4). About 98% of this debt was a long term with a maturity of 13 months or longer, while the remaining 2% was short term. As in most years, roughly 40% of debt municipal debt was issued by states and 60% by local governments. Although municipal debt has more than tripled in nominal terms since the mid-1980s, the change is less dramatic as a percentage of gross domestic product.

Table 3.3 shows the total amount, bond type, bid type, and capital type of municipal bonds sold each year from 1996 to 2020. That total varies from below $200 billion ($182.9 billion in 1996) to just over $480 billion ($484.5 billion in 2020). The annual share of GO bond issuance is in the range of 28.5% and 41.2%. Negotiated sale is the major bid type. The share of new capital in annual municipal bond issuance ranges from a low of 38.2% in 2015 to a high of 82% in 2000.

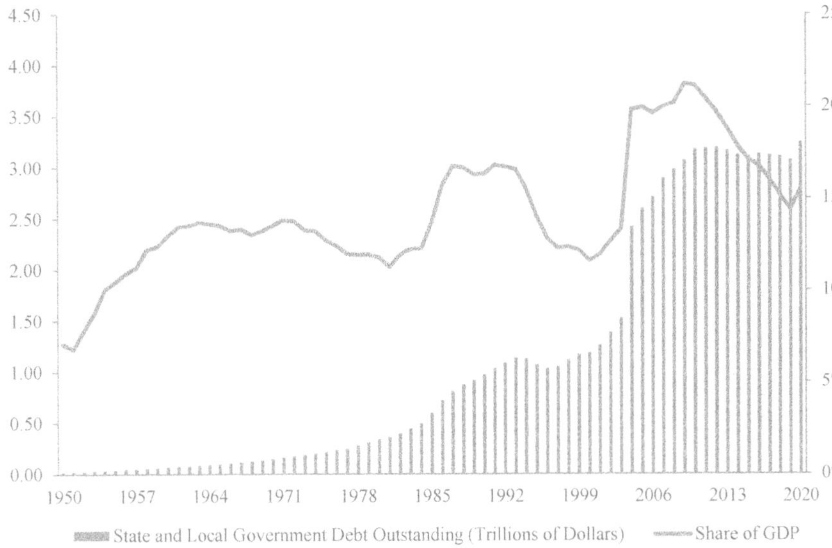

Fig. 3.4 State and local government debt outstanding (1950–2020) (*Data Source* Board of Governors of the Federal Reserve System [U.S.] https://fred.stlouisfed.org/series/SLGSDODNS)

General Obligation Bonds. As mentioned, state and local governments use two general types of bond financing: General Obligation bonds (GO) and revenue bonds. GO bonds are the long-term obligations of state and local governments backed by the issuer's full faith and credit, which means the issuing governments are obligated to repay bonds from their general tax revenues. GO bonds are traditionally issued to finance projects that do not yield substantial revenues, such as public schools, libraries, public safety equipment, city halls, fire stations, and jails. GO bonds usually have better credit ratings and therefore are less costly to bond issuers than revenue bonds. However, GO bonds are often subject to constitutional or statutory debt limits. In many states, they require voter approval. Moreover, GO bonds impose a debt obligation on future taxpayers and limit budget flexibility in future years.

Revenue Bonds. Revenue bonds, also referred to as nonguaranteed debt, are typically issued to finance public facilities that have definable users with specific revenue streams, such as utilities, toll roads and bridges, educational facilities, and hospitals. Revenue bonds are secured by the pledge of defined revenue sources generated from the bond-funded projects (user fees, tolls, facility rent). Revenue bonds generally have more risk due to the uncertainty of generated revenues. Thus, the interest rates for revenue bonds are typically

Table 3.3 Municipal bond issue in USD billions, 1996–2020 (Current dollar)

	Bond type			Bid type				Capital type			Total
	GO	Revenue	%GO	Competitive	Negotiated	Private placement	Percent competitive	New capital	Refunding	% New Capital	Total
1996	63.0	119.9	34.5	46.3	133.0	3.6	25.3	121.7	61.2	66.5	182.9
1997	70.9	147.7	32.4	47.2	165.0	6.5	21.6	135.7	82.9	62.1	218.6
1998	91.3	192.8	32.1	64.2	213.7	6.2	22.6	158.1	126.0	55.7	284.1
1999	68.6	156.0	30.5	51.6	164.9	8.1	23.0	154.5	70.1	68.8	224.6
2000	65.1	133.2	32.8	48.0	144.1	6.2	24.2	162.6	35.6	82.0	198.2
2001	101.1	185.4	35.3	63.0	220.3	3.2	22.0	196.6	89.9	68.6	286.5
2002	124.1	232.6	34.8	71.5	282.3	2.8	20.0	236.1	120.5	66.2	356.6
2003	139.5	240.8	36.7	75.5	302.7	2.1	19.8	257.8	122.5	67.8	380.3
2004	131.5	226.6	36.7	68.4	286.9	2.8	19.1	226.7	131.4	63.3	358.1
2005	144.6	262.5	35.5	75.9	329.4	1.8	18.6	218.9	188.3	53.8	407.1
2006	115.8	272.0	29.9	69.4	312.7	5.8	17.9	256.8	131.1	66.2	387.9
2007	132.6	296.6	30.9	72.7	351.5	5.0	16.9	273.5	155.7	63.7	429.2
2008	110.8	278.5	28.5	53.3	332.8	3.2	13.7	207.5	181.8	53.3	389.3
2009	155.4	254.2	37.9	57.9	348.0	3.7	14.1	260.7	149.0	63.6	409.6
2010	147.5	285.7	34.1	73.2	352.2	7.9	16.9	279.3	154.0	64.5	433.3
2011	106.0	189.1	35.9	59.6	225.7	9.9	20.2	150.4	144.7	51.0	295.1
2012	136.1	246.6	35.6	74.2	295.7	12.8	19.4	148.9	233.7	38.9	382.7
2013	127.9	207.5	38.1	69.4	243.4	22.7	20.7	161.6	173.9	48.2	335.4
2014	136.4	202.8	40.2	71.8	242.8	24.5	21.2	145.4	193.7	42.9	339.1

	Bond type			Bid type				Capital type			Total
	GO	Revenue	%GO	Competitive	Negotiated	Private placement	Percent competitive	New capital	Refunding	% New Capital	Total
2015	158.9	246.2	39.2	87.3	290.1	27.8	21.5	154.6	250.5	38.2	405.1
2016	179.4	272.5	39.7	98.7	325.2	28.1	21.8	176.8	275.1	39.1	451.9
2017	165.2	283.8	36.8	98.2	310.2	40.6	21.9	203.2	245.8	45.2	449.0
2018	123.8	223.0	35.7	82.0	238.4	26.5	23.6	241.8	105.0	69.7	346.8
2019	163.5	262.8	38.4	99.2	307.6	19.6	23.3	264.8	161.6	62.1	426.4
2020	199.6	284.9	41.2	93.0	358.4	33.2	19.2	275.3	209.3	56.8	484.5

Data Source The Securities Industry and Financial Markets Association (SIFMA). (2021). *US-Municipal-Bonds-Statistics-SIFMA*. https://www.sifma.org/resources/research/us-municipal-bonds-statistics/us-municipal-bonds-statistics-sifma/

higher. However, an advantage is that most revenue bonds are not subject to constitutional debt limits and may not require a public vote.

Private Activity Bonds. Private Activity Bonds (PABs) are a type of municipal bond issued by state and local governments on behalf of a private business to build projects that benefit private entities and also serve some public purpose (e.g., airport improvements, water facility upgrades, toll roads). PABs enable private users to benefit from the government's status as a tax-exempt entity and bear lower interest rates. They encourage private sector investment in infrastructure projects with significant public benefits. However, PABs are subject to a federally imposed cap that limits the annual amounts of PABs that can be issued in each state for qualified private activities. Table 3.4 shows the list of 27 qualified private activities. The annual state cap was raised from the greater of \$50 per capita or \$150 million in 2000 to the greater of \$105 per capita or \$311.38 million in 2018 (Maguire & Hughes, 2018).

Leasing-Revenue Bonds. Lease financing (lease purchase of equipment, lease purchase debt, or certificates of participation) has become an increasingly popular bond financing tool used to finance local police vehicles, fire trucks, courthouses, and correctional facilities. A lease between private or nonprofit equipment and facility owners or construction builders (the lessors) transfers the use and ownership of that equipment or facility to a local government (the lessees) for a negotiated period (U.S. Office of the Comptroller of the Currency, 2014). Under a lease agreement, the lessors use the regular lease payments from the local government to repay debt service. Interest income on a municipal lease is tax-exempt to the lessor. At the end of the lease period, the local government often assumes ownership of the property. Lease financing has no required bond referendum and is not subject to legal debt limits. Therefore, it has greater flexibility. However, lease payments require an annual budgetary appropriation. Where there is not a multiple-year appropriation or dedicated revenue source to secure lease payments, lease financing has a higher interest rate.

3.4 Key Principles for Infrastructure Finance

Previous section discusses the various types of traditional infrastructure funding and financing methods. Different infrastructure financing mechanisms are appropriate for different types of infrastructure projects, scales

Table 3.4 List of qualified private activities authorized by the U.S. federal governments

Internal Revenue Code Section	Type of Private Activity (Italicized activities must be owned by the issuing government to qualify)	Subject to Volume Cap	Year Established
§142	**Exempt facility bonds**		
§142(c)	*Airports*	No	1968
§142(c)	*Docks and wharves*	No	1968
§142(c)	*Mass commuting facilities*	Yes	1981
§142(e)	Water furnishing facilities	Yes	1968
§142(a)(5)	Sewage facilities	Yes	1968
§142(a)(6)	Solid waste disposal facilities (government owned)	No	1968
§142(a)(6)	Solid waste disposal facilities (private owned)	Yes	1968
§142(d)	Qualified residential rental projects	Yes	1968
§142(f)	Local electric energy or gas furnishing facility	Yes	1968
§142(g)	Local district heating and cooling facilities	Yes	1982
§142(h)	Qualified hazardous waste facilities	Yes	1986
§142(l)	High-speed intercity rail facilities (government)	No	1988
§142(l)	High-speed intercity rail facilities (private)	Yes	1988
§142(j)	*Environmental enhancements of hydroelectric generating facilities*	No	1992

(continued)

Table 3.4 (continued)

Internal Revenue Code Section	Type of Private Activity (Italicized activities must be owned by the issuing government to qualify)	Subject to Volume Cap	Year Established
§142(k)	Qualified public educational facilities	No	2001
§142(l)	Qualified green building and sustainable design projects	No	2005
§142(m)	Qualified highway and surface freight transfer facilities	No	2005
§1400U-3	Recovery zone facility bonds	No	2009
§1394	New empowerment zone facilities	No	1994
§143	**Mortgage revenue bonds**		
§143(a)	Qualified mortgage bond	No	1968
§143(b)	Qualified veterans' mortgage bond	Yes	1968
§144(a)	Qualified small issue bond	Yes	1968
§144(b)	Qualified student loan bond	Yes	1976
§144(c)	Qualified redevelopment bond	Yes	1968
§145	Qualified 501(c)(3) bond	No	1968
§150	Current refunding bonds not exceeding outstanding amount of refunding bonds	No	1968

(continued)

Table 3.4 (continued)

Internal Revenue Code Section	Type of Private Activity (Italicized activities must be owned by the issuing government to qualify)	Subject to Volume Cap	Year Established
§150	Current refunding bonds exceeding outstanding amount of refunding bonds	Yes	1968

Source Maguire and Hughes (2018, p. 10)

of funding needed, and types of entity. These mechanisms are related. For instance, revenues from taxes and user fees can be used to repay bonds. There are key principles for evaluating and choosing infrastructure financing mechanisms:

- *Revenue adequacy*: the ability to generate sufficient revenues that are predictable and stable to match the timing, scale, and the purpose of the specific infrastructure projects.
- *Administrative simplicity*: easy, inexpensive, and less complicated for the governments to administer.
- *Economic effectiveness:* incur a low cost of capital including associated transaction costs.
- *Attract and stimulate private investment:* leveraging public funding to mobilize private capital and tap into private sector's expertise and innovation.
- *Fairness and equity:* Fairness means the cost burden of infrastructure development broadly reflects benefits provided by geography, risk reduction, and others. Equity means that the cost burden reflects the ability to pay.
- *Appropriate alignment of incentives:* align incentives to overcome marker failures and facilitate flow of capital to projects where the aggregate benefits exceed the costs.
- *Political feasibility:* political acceptability to a broad set of stakeholders.

References

Anderson, J. E. (2012). *Public finance*. Cengage Learning.

Bunch, B. S. (2012). Capital planning and budgeting. in J.R. Bartle, W.B., Hildreth, & J. Marlowe (Ed.), *Management policies in local government finance* (pp. 253–278). International City/County Management Association Press.

Bartle, J. R., & Chen, C. (2015). Future issues in state transportation finance. In K. G. Willoughby & M. M. Rubin (Eds.), *Sustaining the states: The Fiscal viability of American state governments* (pp. 211–234). Taylor & Francis Group Press.

Fisher, R. C. (2007). *State and local public finance* (3rd ed.). Thomson.

Fisher, R. C. (2016). *State and local public finance* (4th ed.). Routledge.

Kelly, L. (2016). *The danger in using bank loans to fund infrastructure*.http://www.govtech.com/fs/perspectives/The-Danger-in-Using-Bank-Loans-to-Fund-Infrastructure.html. Accessed 3 August 2021.

International City/County Management Association (ICMA). (2017). *Innovations and emerging practices in local government 2016 survey: Summary report of results.* https://icma.org/sites/default/files/309068_ICMA%20Innovation%20Survey%20Summary%20Report.pdf. Accessed 1 August 2021.

Lee Jr, R. D., Johnson, R. W., & Joyce, P. G. (2021). *Public budgeting systems.* Jones & Bartlett Learning.

Lobosco, K. & Luhby, T. (2021, November 5). Here's What's in the Bipartisan Infrastructure Bill. *CNN*. https://www.cnn.com/2021/07/28/politics/infrastructure-bill-explained/index.html. Accessed on 8 November 2021.

Maguire, S., & Hughes, J. S. (2018). *Private activity bonds: An introduction.* https://fas.org/sgp/crs/misc/RL31457.pdf. Accessed 3 August 2021.

Mallett, W.J. (2020). *Transportation infrastructure investment as economic stimulus: Lessons from the American recovery and reinvestment act of 2009.* US Congressional Research Service. https://fas.org/sgp/crs/misc/R46343.pdf.Accessed. Accessed 1 August 2021.

Marlowe, J., Rivenbark, W. C., & Vogt, A. J. (2009). *Capital budgeting and finance: A guide for local governments.* International City/County Management Association Press.

Marlowe, J. (2015). *Municipal bonds and infrastructure development—Past, present, and future. A Policy Issue White Paper Prepared on behalf of the ICMA Governmental Affairs and Policy Committee.* http://icma.org/en/icma/knowledge_network/documents/kn/Document/307554/Municipal_Bonds_and_Infrastructure_Development__Past_Present_and_Future. Accessed 3 August 2021.

Metropolitan Government of Nashville and Davidson County. (2020). *30003 4% reserve fund—At a glance*. https://filetransfer.nashville.gov/portals/0/sitecontent/Finance/docs/OMB/fy21_budget/Recommended/30003-4PercentReserveFund.pdf. Accessed 7 December 2021.

Tax Policy Center. (2020). *What are municipal bonds and how are they used?* https://www.taxpolicycenter.org/briefing-book/what-are-municipal-bonds-and-how-are-they-used. Accessed 1 August 2021.

The California Debt and Investment Advisory Commission. (2021). *California debt financing guide*. https://www.treasurer.ca.gov/cdiac/debtpubs/financing-guide.pdf. Accessed 1 August 2021.

The Congressional Budget Office (CBO). (2015). *Estimated impact of the American Recovery and Reinvestment Act on employment and economic output in 2014*. https://www.cbo.gov/sites/default/files/114th-congress-2015-2016/reports/49958-ARRA.pdf

The Securities Industry and Financial Markets Association (SIFMA). (2021). *US-Municipal-Bonds-Statistics-SIFMA*. https://www.sifma.org/resources/research/us-municipal-bonds-statistics/us-municipal-bonds-statistics-sifma/. Accessed 7 December 2021.

The White House. (2021). *Fact sheet: The American job plan*. https://www.whitehouse.gov/briefing-room/statements-releases/2021/03/31/fact-sheet-the-american-jobs-plan/. Accessed 3 August 2021.

U.S. Board of Governor of the Federal Reserve System. (2021). *Z.1 financial accounts of the United States units: Billions of dollars, seasonally adjusted*. https://fred.stlouisfed.org/series/SLGSDODNS. Accessed 16 November 2021.

U.S. Census Bureau. (2021). *Annual state and local government finances summary: 2019*. https://www.census.gov/library/publications/2019/econ/g19-alfin-summary.html. Accessed 1 August 2021.

U.S. Congress. (2021). *H.R.3684—Infrastructure investment and jobs act*. https://www.congress.gov/bill/117th-congress/house-bill/3684. Accessed 21 November 2021.

U.S. Congressional Research Service. (2015). *The demand for municipal bonds: Issues for congress*. https://crsreports.congress.gov/product/pdf/R/R44146. Accessed 7 December 2021

U.S. Department of Transportation. (2015). *The fixing America's surface transportation act or "FAST Act"*. https://www.transportation.gov/fastac. Accessed 27 September 2021

U.S. Office of the Comptroller of the Currency. (2014). *Leasing finance*. http://www.occ.treas.gov/publications/publications-by-type/comptrollers-handbook/pub-ch-lease-financing.pdf. Accessed 1 August 2021.

Wang, W., Hou, Y., & Duncombe, W. (2007). Determinants of pay-as-you-go financing of capital projects: Evidence from the states. *Public Budgeting & Finance, 27*(4), 18–42.

Wang, W., & Hou, Y. (2009). Pay-as-you-go financing and capital outlay volatility: Evidence from the states over two recent economic cycles. *Public Budgeting & Finance, 29*(4), 90–107.

WM Financial Strategies. (n.d.). *Bond sale methods*. https://www.munibondadvisor.com/SaleChoice.htm. Accessed 12 September 2021.

4

Innovative Mechanisms of Financing Infrastructure

This chapter describes three types of innovative infrastructure financing. The first section pinpoints the need for innovative infrastructure finance. The second section defines innovative infrastructure financing and describes its three types: new funding sources, new financing mechanisms, and new financial arrangements. The following three sections further depict various new funding sources, new financing mechanisms, and new financial arrangements, respectively.

4.1 The Need for Innovative Infrastructure Finance

Every four years, the American Society of Civil Engineers (ASCE) publishes the Report Card for America's Infrastructure, which grades the current state of national infrastructure categories on a scale of A through F. As indicated in Table 4.1, since 1988, America's infrastructure has consistently received low grades. Over the next ten years, the estimated infrastructure investment needs have grown from $1.3 trillion in 2001 to $5.9 trillion in 2021. Besides the ASCE, the U.S. Environmental Protection Agency (EPA)'s 6th Drinking Water Infrastructure Needs Survey and Assessment shows that more than $470 billion is needed to maintain and improve the nation's drinking water infrastructure over the next 20 years (U.S. EPA, 2018).

C. Chen and J. R. Bartle, *Innovative Infrastructure Finance*,
https://doi.org/10.1007/978-3-030-91411-0_4

Table 4.1 The American Society of Civil Engineers (ASCE) Infrastructure Report Card history

Category	1988	1998	2001	2005	2009	2013	2017	2021
Aviation	B–	C–	D	D+	D	D	D	D+
Bridges	N/A	C–	C	C	C	C+	C+	C
Dams	N/A	D	D	D+	D	D	D	D
Drinking Water	B–	D	D	D	D–	D	D	C–
Energy	N/A	N/A	D+	D	D+	D+	D+	C–
Hazardous Waste	D	D–	D+	D	D	D	D+	D+
Inland Waterways	B–	N/A	D+	D–	D–	D–	D	D+
Levees	N/A	N/A	N/A	N/A	D–	D–	D	D
Ports	N/A	N/A	N/A	N/A	N/A	C	C+	B–
Public Parks	N/A	N/A	N/A	C–	C–	C–	D+	D+
Rail	N/A	N/A	N/A	C–	C–	C+	B	B
Roads	C+	D–	D+	D	D–	D	D	D
Schools	D	F	D–	D	D	D	D+	D+
Solid Waste	C–	C–	C+	C+	C+	B–	C+	C+
Storm Water	N/A	N/A	N/A	N/A	N/A	N/A	D	D
Transit	C–	C	C–	D+	D	D	D–	D–
Wastewater	C	D+	D	D–	D–	D	D+	D+
Overall GPA	C	D	D+	D	D	D+	D+	C–
Investment Needs Over 10 Years	N/A	N/A	$1.3 Trillion	$1.6 Trillion	$2.2 Trillion	$3.6 Trillion	$4.6 Trillion	$5.9 Trillion

Note The national infrastructure report card originated in 1988 with the congressionally charted National Council on Public Works Improvement report—*Fragile Foundations: A Report on America's Public Works.* ASCE published its first Report Card on America's Infrastructure in 1998. The infrastructure report card grading scale is the following: A (exceptional, fit for the future), B (good, adequate for now), C (mediocre, requires attention), D (poor, at risk), and F (failing/critical unfit for purpose). https://infrastructurereportcard.org/making-the-grade/

Data Source ASCE's 2021 Infrastructure Report Card

The latest 2021 Report Card for America's Infrastructure gives the nation's critical infrastructure an overall grade of C– (ASCE, 2021). The disaggregated grades for different infrastructure systems range from the highest grade (B for rail) to the lowest grade (D+ for aviation, hazardous waste, inland waterways, public parks and recreation, schools, and wastewater). ASCE (2021) estimated an infrastructure investment gap of $2.6 trillion between 2020 and 2029. The surface transportation system experiences the largest funding gap of $1.215 trillion. The second largest funding gap is water/wastewater/stormwater ($434 billion). The third largest funding gap is schools ($380 billion). ASCE (2021) estimates that the failure of closing this gap could cost the nation almost $10.3 trillion in gross domestic product as well as a loss of 3 million jobs through 2039. By 2039, America's overdue infrastructure bill will cost the average American household $3,300 a year, or $63 a week.

In the U.S., public officials at all levels of government are challenged to identify sufficient revenue resources and cost-effective ways to fund and finance the needs of preserving and improving the current public infrastructure system (see Table 4.2). Although traditional taxes and fees still play the dominant role in funding public infrastructure, these revenues have not kept pace with the investment demands of an aging and deteriorating American public infrastructure system. For instance, due to improved fuel economy and rising construction and maintenance costs, federal motor fuel taxes have lost purchasing power and become the least sustainable highway revenue source. Moreover, state and local budgets are strained by competing demands of public employee pensions and rising healthcare costs.

Table 4.2 Cumulative infrastructure investment funding gap for 2020–2029 (billions)

Category	Total needs	Funded	Funded gap
Surface Transportation	$2,834	$1,619	$1,215
Water/Wastewater/Stormwater	$1,045	$611	$434
Electricity	$637	$440	$197
Airports	$237	$126	$111
Inland Waterways & Marine Ports	$42	$17	$25
Dams	$93.60	$12.50	$81
Hazardous & Solid Waste	$21	$14.40	$7
Levees	$80	$10.10	$70
Public Parks & Recreation	$77.50	$9.50	$68
Schools	$870	$490	$380
Totals	$5,937	$3,350	$2,588

Data Source ASCE's 2021 Infrastructure Report Card

Addressing the public infrastructure financing challenges is a critical undertaking for the nation. Bridging the large infrastructure funding gaps requires creativity and innovation in the design, planning, funding, financing, construction, and operations and maintenance of infrastructure assets. The need for more creative ways of financing public infrastructure investments is well-documented and supported by all levels of government agencies and other stakeholders. The U.S. Department of Treasury (2014) calls for expanding the nation's infrastructure through innovative financing by stating that "*Notwithstanding the United States' deep municipal bond market, innovative financing for infrastructure investment is becoming increasingly important as public budgets continue to tighten at all levels of government*" (p. 8, emphasis original). Former President Obama launched the Build America Investment Initiative in July 2014, calling on increasing investment in U.S. roads, ports, and drinking water systems through innovative financing, particularly facilitating partnerships between federal, state, and local governments and private sector investors (The White House, 2014). The Water Infrastructure Finance and Innovation Act of 2014 (WIFIA) established the WIFIA program, a federal credit program administered by EPA for eligible water and wastewater infrastructure projects. The Fixing Americas Surface Transportation (FAST) Act created the National Surface Transportation and Innovative Finance Bureau, a new office intended to help promote the use of innovative finance programs in the U.S. Department of Transportation. ASCE Policy Statement 496 (2019) also supports innovative financing programs for transportation projects and advocates making programs available in all states.

4.2 An Overview of Innovative Infrastructure Finance

In response to the declining financial resources for building infrastructure, a set of innovative finance mechanisms has been utilized by governments at all three levels to complement the conventional methods of infrastructure finance. *So, what is innovative infrastructure finance?* There is no standard definition of the term. Chen (2016a) defines innovative infrastructure finance as an umbrella concept that supplements traditional infrastructure funding sources and financing methods and embraces any strategy involving new funding sources, new financing mechanisms, and new financial arrangements in the provision of public infrastructure (Fig. 4.1).

Using Chen's (2016a) definition, we categorize innovative infrastructure finance into three types (see Table 4.3):

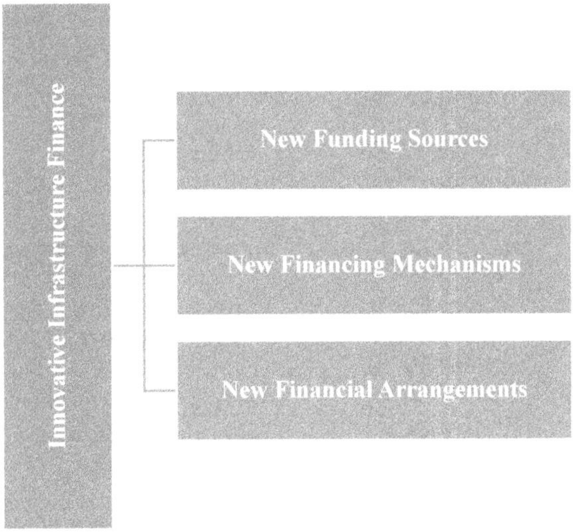

Fig. 4.1 Innovative infrastructure finance: A conceptual framework (*Source* The Authors)

- *New funding sources* are any new measure that generates additional revenue to pay for infrastructure projects. They include new taxes such as local option taxes that are earmarked for infrastructure projects, or different value capture mechanisms such as impact fees or development exactions, which are charged to compensate the cost of constructing new infrastructure improvement projects during the development process.
- *New financing mechanisms* represent new methods for borrowing money in flexible and/or potentially cost-effective ways to pay for an infrastructure project. They include new credit assistance tools (loans, loan guarantees, and lines of credit) offered by governments and alternative bond and debt financing tools (GARVEE [Grant Anticipation Revenue Vehicle] bonds, green bonds, and environmental impact bonds).
- *New financial arrangements* involve new partners (the private sector, the nonprofit sector, or the public) to participate in infrastructure financing and project delivery.

Table 4.3 Typology and categories of innovative infrastructure finance

New Funding Sources	New Taxes	Local Option Taxes
		VMT Tax
		Electric Vehicle Taxes
		Carbon Taxes
	New Fees	Value Capture
		Resilience Fees
New Financing Mechanisms	New Credit Assistance Tools (Loan, Loan Guarantee, Lines of Credit)	Transportation Infrastructure Finance and Innovation Act (TIFIA) Loans
		Water Infrastructure Finance and Innovation Act (WIFIA)
		Environmental State Revolving Funds
		State Infrastructure Banks
	New Bonds and Debt Financing Tools	Grant Anticipation Revenue Vehicle Bonds (GARVEEs)
		Green Bonds
		Catastrophe Bonds and Resilience Bonds
		Environmental Impact Bond
New Financial Arrangements	Public–Private Partnerships	Design-Build
		Design-Build-Operate-Maintain
		Design-Build-Finance-Operate-Maintain
		Concession
	Privatization	Lease/Asset Recycling
	Infrastructure Investment Funds	Pension Funds
		Sovereign Wealth Funds
		Private Companies (Insurance and Investment Banks)
	Private and Nonprofit Philanthropic Partners	Donations
		Grants
		Program Investment
	Crowdfunding	Donation-Based (Public Goods)

Note This table is not intended to be inclusive of all innovative mechanisms but instead inventories and assesses a series of key creative and emerging ways of paying for infrastructure
Source The Authors

4.3 New Funding Sources

4.3.1 New Taxes: Local Option Taxes

Description: In response to declining fiscal resources for infrastructure projects, local governments are searching for new revenue sources to fund their infrastructure needs. One option available in many states is to adopt local option taxes (Chen & Afonso, 2021). Local option taxes are new tax options that are either authorized at the state level or approved by local voters and levied at the county or municipal level for infrastructure-related purposes (Chen & Afonso, 2021; Goldman & Wachs, 2003). The most common forms of local option taxes are local option sales tax (LOST), and states such as Arizona, California, Minnesota, and Texas have LOSTs earmarked for transportation purposes. In addition to LOSTs, some states authorize other types of local option taxes, such as local option fuel tax (LOFT), local option vehicle tax (LOVT), and local option income or payroll taxes (LOITs). Revenues from local option taxes are sometimes earmarked for building special local infrastructure projects.

With the property tax and other local revenues are often limited by state laws, local governments across the U.S. have increasingly turned to local option taxes to fund transportation projects.

Local Option Taxes

According to the National League of Cities (NLC), 29 states authorize a LOST, 16 states authorize a LOFT, 26 states authorize LOVT, and 17 states authorize LOITs (NLC, 2016; Walczak, 2019).

- **Local Option Sales Tax (LOST)** is a special purpose tax implemented and levied at the city or county level. LOSTs are always appended onto the base state sales tax rate. States vary in how they delegate spending authority for LOSTs.
- **Local Option Fuels Tax (LOFT)** is a special purpose tax implemented and levied at the city or county level on motor fuel. These taxes are generally earmarked for transportation-related purpose.
- **Local Option Vehicle Tax (LOVT)** is a tax implemented and levied at the city or county level as either a vehicle registration fee or annual taxes on vehicle value, weight, age, body type, or number of wheels.
- **Local Option Income/ Payroll Taxes** (LOITs) are a tax implemented and levied at the city or county level as a percentage of salaries or wages, a percentage of state or federal income taxes, or as a flat charge per week. The tax may be paid by individuals or employers.

Source National League of Cities. (2016). *Paying for local infrastructure in a new era of federalism*. https://www.nlc.org/wp-content/uploads/2016/12/NLC_2016_Infrastructure_Report.pdf; Walczak, J. (2019). *Local income taxes in 2019*. https://files.taxfoundation.org/20190730170302/Local-Income-Taxes-in-20191.pdf.

Advantages and Disadvantages: The main advantages of local option taxes include that they are transparent and democratically approved, dedicated to specific projects with local priorities and fairly stable and predictable revenue sources. However, the significant disadvantages of local option taxes are that they require direct voter approval, are often subject to rate limitations and spending restrictions, and may favor capital construction over regular maintenance activities.

Examples: Local government reliance on local option tax revenues is increasing. Voters in cities including Atlanta, Charlotte, Dallas, Denver, Seattle, and St. Louis have approved the use of a local option sales tax for constructing new rail projects. For instance, on November 8, 2016, Atlanta citizens voted in favor of a special purpose local option sales tax for transportation (T-SPLOST) for four-tenths of a penny or an additional 4 cents on a $10 purchase. This T-SPLOST was estimated to yield nearly $300 million over a five-year period to fund significant and expansive transportation projects (The City of Atlanta, 2016).

In Florida, all counties are eligible to levy up to 12 cents of LOFTs in three separate levies on fuel sold within the county. LOFTs represent a significant revenue source to fund Florida's local transportation infrastructure. In fiscal year 2017, the total amount of LOFT revenue statewide was $920 million, which accounted for close to 30% of local transportation funding sources in the state of Florida (Chen & Afonso, 2021). In 2015, Osceola County (Florida) commissioners approved a 5 cent per gallon local gas tax increase which was estimated to yield about $6 million per year for use on road capital improvement and maintenance.

In 2016, voters in Marion County, Indiana, approved a referendum that authorizes the city of Indianapolis to impose an income tax of up to 0.25% (25 cents per $100 of income) to help fund the Marion County Transit Plan—$390 million in improvements to improve regional bus service (Litman, 2021).

In Wisconsin, local governments have the option to levy a local vehicle registration fee (wheel tax) in addition to the state $75 registration fees for most vehicles. State law requires local governments to use the funding for local transportation projects. In 2011, only four local governments had such a tax in place. By the end of 2017, 27 local governments adopt this tax (Wisconsin Policy Forum, 2018). The wheel tax revenues nearly tripled from $7.1 million in 2011 to $20.7 million in 2017 (Wisconsin Policy Forum, 2018) (Table 4.4).

Table 4.4 Characteristics of four common local option taxes

Equity	Sales	Fuel	Vehicle	Income
Do all households pay?	Yes	No	No	Yes
Is the tax regressive?	Yes	Yes	Yes	No
Do non-residents contribute?	Yes	Yes	No	Yes
Stability				
Broad tax base?	Broad	Narrow	Narrow	Broad
Indexed for inflation?	Yes	No	No	Yes
Fluctuates with economy?	Yes	Some	No	Some
Transportation Relevance				
Relevance to highways	Weak	Strong	Strong	Weak
Relevance to streets?	Weak	Strong	Strong	Weak
Relevance to transit?	Moderate	Moderate	Moderate	Moderate
Typical Applications				
Types of projects funded	Highway/Transit Capital & Operation	Highway Capital & Mainte-nance	Highway Capital & mainte-nance	Transit Operation
Typical tax rate	0.25%	5 cents per gallon	\$10–\$20 per vehicle	0.0025
Typical revenues per capita	\$30–\$60	\$20–\$35	\$7.0–\$8.5	\$30–\$60

Source Goldman et al. (2001, p. 21)

4.3.2 New Taxes: VMT Tax

Description: In the U.S., the primary source of transportation funding is the motor fuel tax. However, as vehicles have become increasingly fuel-efficient, gasoline taxes have lagged in terms of both inflation-adjusted rates and revenues sufficient to fund America's highway systems. An innovative approach to solving the long-term funding issue for sustainable transportation is to replace the fuel tax with a Vehicle-Mile Traveled (VMT) tax. A VMT tax is also referred to as a VMT fee, a mileage-based user fee (MBUF), a road usage charge (RUC), or per-mile tax. In general, a VMT tax charges drivers based on distance driven (Agrawal et al., 2016). This tax directly relates to road usage as opposed to the fuel tax, which is based on fuel consumed. The per-mile tax rate can be varied based on the vehicle type and weight, location, emission, and congestion of the road system on which the vehicle travels (Agrawal et al., 2016).

While increasing the gas tax may be a viable short-term strategy, implementing the VMT tax is widely considered a long-term strategy. A report of the National Surface Transportation Infrastructure Commission (2009) recommends the VMT tax as a new approach to funding transportation infrastructure. Oregon was the first state to enact a bill to study road user charges to replace its gas tax in 2001. Other states have subsequently introduced their own VMT legislation. In 2019 and 2020, 19 states (Hawaii, Idaho, Illinois, Iowa, Kentucky, Maine, Maryland, Massachusetts, Michigan, Minnesota, Nevada, New Mexico, New York, Oregon, Texas, Utah, Vermont, Virginia, and Washington) considered 34 pieces of legislation addressing the VMT tax. Of those, seven states (Maine, Nevada, New Mexico, Oregon, Utah, Virginia, and Washington) enacted eight pieces of legislation (NCSL, 2021a).

Advantages and Disadvantages: The primary advantages of a VMT tax include: (1) yielding greater economic efficiency by closely linking transportation taxes to the actual use of the roadways and encouraging drivers to ration their travel behavior, (2) protecting transportation funding from technological advances in fuel efficiency, and (3) generating long-term revenue stability. The downsides of VMT tax include: (1) the privacy concerns in collecting the tax, especially if location data is collected, (2) a costly and complex collection and administering system, and (3) difficulty of enforcement.

Examples: Since the early twentieth century, Oregon has been a leader in implementing the user-pay principle in road finance. In 1919, Oregon became the first state that adopted a gasoline tax. Since 2000, technological advances in the automobile industry have stimulated the growing sales of hybrid and electric cars. Anticipating the widespread adoption of these fuel-efficient new vehicles in future, the state legislature in Oregon began to seek a more equitable and efficient alternative road funding source. In 2001, an independent Road User Fee Task Force was created by the state legislature with the mission to design a feasible alternative to the motor fuel tax.

In 2006, the Oregon Department of Transportation (ODOT) launched the first pilot study on the feasibility of the VMT implementation. The VMT alternative is a pay-at-the-pump model for mileage charging, using government-selected mileage reporting devices installed in vehicles to measure distance traveled and report mileage data to electronic data readers installed in fuel pumps. The mileage data contains information about the location and number of miles driven. The central servers at the fuel stations process the mileage data stored at the electronic data readers and automatically calculate and send drivers the road use charge as a part of the normal process of gas purchase transaction (ODOT, 2007). Despite the feasibility of the pay-at-the-pump model, the mandate of GPS-based mileage reporting devices raised privacy concerns about tracking information about driving locations.

In 2012, ODOT launched the second pilot study on the viability of the VMT implementation, to deal with the privacy concern. The second VMT pilot program incorporated the most recent smartphone wireless communication for reporting mileage and managing payments (ODOT, 2007). Compared with the pay-at-the-pump model for mileage charging, the second VMT program relied upon the open system structure with adaptability to multiple providers (rather than the government provider). There is no mandate for location-based GPS technology except by driver choice. In addition, drivers have multiple choices for reporting and account payment mechanisms. About 90 motorists from three states and two private vendors participated in the second program. The second VMT pilot program received positive evaluations. It addressed the issue of privacy and achieved the goals of ease of use, motorist choices, open system, and private sector management. Participants were charged 1.56 cents per mile, and the total VMT fees collected exceeded fuel tax revenues by about 28% (ODOT, 2007). Following the success of the second VMT fee pilot program, Oregon's state legislature passed Senate Bill 810 and established the nation's first mileage-based revenue program (OreGO) for light vehicles. Beginning July 1, 2015, 5000 volunteers were charged 1.50 cents per mile driven (ODOT, 2007).

4.3.3 New Taxes: Electric Vehicle Tax

Description: According to the Edison Electric Institute (2018), annual sales of electric vehicles (EVs) will exceed 3.5 million vehicles in 2030, reaching more than 20% of annual vehicle sales. The number of EVs on U.S. roads is projected to reach 18.7 million in 2030, up from 1 million in 2018 (Edison Electric Institute, 2018). An electric vehicle consumes no taxed motor fuels. The growth of EV sales will result in a significant loss of gas tax revenue.

Recently, many states across the U.S. are introducing an electric vehicle tax to make up for lost gas tax revenue. An electric vehicle tax is an annual

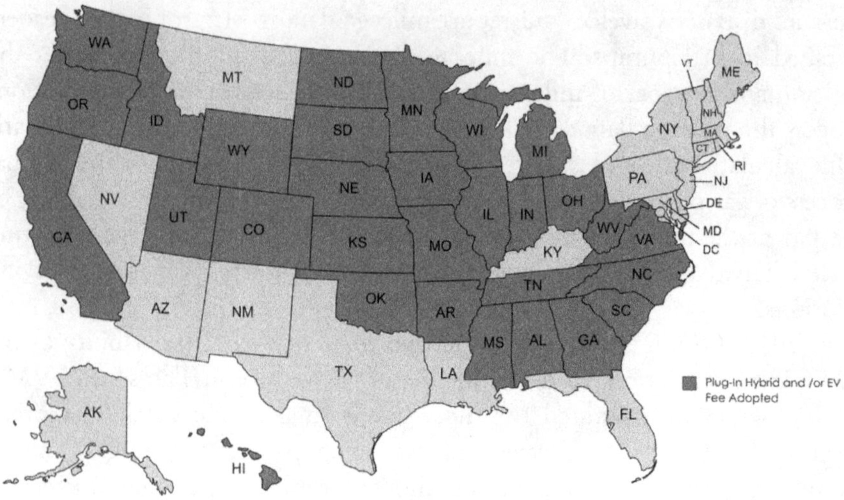

Fig. 4.2 State Plug-in Hybrid and/or Electric Vehicles Tax/Fee (as of October 2021) (*Data Source* NCSL [2021b]. Special Fees on Plug-In Hybrid and Electric Vehicles. https://www.ncsl.org/research/energy/new-fees-on-hybrid-and-electric-vehicles.aspx)

registration tax or fee imposed on the owners of electric vehicles (US Congressional Research Service, 2020). As indicated in Fig. 4.2, as of October 2021, 30 states had adopted an EV tax or fee (or plug-in hybrid and electric vehicles).[1] An EV tax varies considerably across the states, ranging from a low of $50 in Colorado, South Dakota, and Hawaii to a high of $225 in Washington state (NCSL, 2021b). The EV tax can be determined based on a formula that approximates how much an EV owner would pay in gas taxes if they drove a comparable conventional vehicle. In most cases, revenues from the EV tax are directed toward a state transportation fund. However, a few states allocate a portion of the EV tax revenues to fund electric vehicle infrastructure. For instance, Alabama allocates $50 of its $200 eV tax for new electric vehicle infrastructure. Colorado dedicates $20 of the $50 eV tax to the Electric Vehicle Grand Fund, which is used to support charging stations.

Advantages and Disadvantages: The main strengths of the EV tax are: (1) it is not affected by increases in fuel efficiency, (2) it affects all registered vehicle owners equally regardless of their road use, (3) it makes up the loss of gas tax revenue from the growing sales of EVs, and (4) its low cost to implement. Its main disadvantages are: (1) continued concerns about privacy, (2) general

[1] According to NCSL (2021b), hybrid and electric vehicles consist of the following categories: plug-in electric vehicles (PEV), battery electric vehicles (BEV), plug-in hybrid electric vehicles (PHEV), and hybrid electric vehicles (HEV).

opposition to tax or fee increases, and (3) the tax may discourage the purchase of EVs, conflicting with the promotion of energy efficiency.

Examples: EV owners in Colorado must pay an annual fee of $50 for a Plug-in Electric and Electric Vehicle Decal. The annual fee contributes to two funds, with $30 going to the Highway Users Tax Fund and $20 to the Electric Vehicle Grant Fund.

The Nebraska Department of Motor Vehicles (DMV) imposes an annual fee of $75 on any vehicle powered by a source not otherwise subject to state motor fuel tax, including electricity. The Nebraska DMV collects the fee at the time of initial vehicle registration and regular renewal.

In 2015, Georgia began to charge a $200 annual license fee for non-commercial alternative fueled vehicles. The fee is automatically adjusted on an annual basis.

4.3.4 New Taxes: Carbon Taxes

In the U.S., the transportation sector is the largest contributor to greenhouse gas emissions. According to U.S. Environmental Protection Agency (EPA), in 2018, over 28% of carbon dioxide (CO_2) emissions were generated from the transportation sector (EPA, 2020). Greenhouse gas emissions from transportation mainly come from burning fossil fuels (e.g., gasoline, diesel) for passenger vehicles, trucks, trains, ships, and planes. Considering the growing challenges of global warming and climate change, advocates have proposed adopting a revenue-neutral carbon tax to curb transportation carbon emissions.

In general, a carbon tax takes the form of a tax on the consumption of energy products (Brill, 2017). This tax could be designed as an addition to the current fuel tax rate based on the varying carbon context of different fuels. While the main motivation for a carbon tax is to reduce carbon emission, if implemented, the tax revenue raised can be used to support infrastructure. Finland and Sweden implemented carbon taxes during the 1990s. Quebec and British Columbia introduced the first carbon tax in North America in 2007 and 2008, respectively. Both provinces continue to tax gasoline for motor vehicles. The City of Boulder, Colorado, applied a carbon tax to electricity generation beginning in 2007. Several U.S. states have discussed levying a carbon tax. However, to date, none have adopted this tax.

Advantages and Disadvantages: The main advantages of the carbon tax are: (1) providing additional funds to help reduce traffic congestion, (2) reducing negative environmental externalities of transportation use, and (3) enhancing greater economic efficiency by encouraging consumers to voluntarily reduce fuel consumption. The disadvantages include: (1) public opposition to tax increases and (2) the revenue generated by the carbon tax could be eroded by increased fuel efficiency.

Examples: On July 1, 2008, the Canadian province of British Columbia (BC) adopted the first carbon tax in North America. The tax was initially levied at C$10 per ton of carbon dioxide equivalent. It then rose C$5 per ton each year until 2012, when it reached C$30 per ton. The current carbon tax rate maintains the level of C$30 per ton (equivalent to US$24 per ton). The taxed fuels include liquid transportation fuels, such as gasoline and diesel fuel, as well as natural gas or coal used to power electric plants.

One unique aspect of BC's carbon tax as designed was its revenue neutrality. The carbon tax operates as a tax shift in which carbon tax revenues are countered by cuts in other taxes or direct transfers to households rather than raising taxes and increasing government expenditure. Between its inception in 2008 and 2015, the BC carbon tax has yield C$6.1 billion in revenue while the corresponding tax cuts have been more than C$7.1 billion (Murray & Rivers, 2015). Empirical models suggest that this carbon tax has reduced emissions in the province by 5 to 15% (Murray & Rivers, 2015).

4.3.5 New Fees: Value Capture

Description: Value capture refers to "a set of techniques that generally take advantage of increases in property values, economic activity, and growth linked to infrastructure investments to help fund current or future improvements" (U.S. DOT, 2019, p. 1). With value capture, those who benefit from a new infrastructure investment—including property owners or developers—pay for some of its costs, which shifts part of the funding burden away from taxpayers. The common examples of value capture strategies include tax increment financing (TIF), special assessments, joint development, transportation utility fees, developer contributions, and naming rights. Table 4.5 presents the definitions of common value capture techniques. Table 4.6 summarizes the main features of common value capture techniques.

Advantages and Disadvantages: The major advantages of value capture are: (1) shifting the burden of infrastructure finance from the general public to the properties that directly receive the benefit, (2) matching payments with benefits, (3) no requirement of voter approval, and (4) attracting and stimulating private sector investment. The main disadvantages of value capture include: (1) administration and assessment burden, (2) it may only partially

Table 4.5 Overview of value capture categories, techniques, and definitions

Category	Technique	Definition
Developer Contributions	Impact Fees	Fees imposed on developers to help fund additional public services, infrastructure, or transportation facilities required due to the new development
	Negotiated Exactions	Negotiated charges imposed on developers to mitigate the cost of public services or infrastructure required as a result of the new development
Transportation Utility Fees	Transportation Utility Fees	Fees paid by property owners or building occupants to a municipality based on estimated use of the transportation system
	Special Assessment Districts	Fees charged on property owners within a designated district whose properties are the primary beneficiaries of an infrastructure improvement
Special Taxes and Fees	Business Improvement Districts	Fees or levies charged on businesses within a designated district to fund or finance projects or services within the district's boundaries
	Land Value Taxes	Split tax rates, where a higher tax rate is imposed on land than on buildings
	Sales Tax Districts	Additional sales taxes levied on all transactions or purchases in a designated area that benefits from an infrastructure improvement
Tax Increment Financing	Tax Increment Financing	Charges that capture incremental property tax value increases from an investment in a designated district to fund or finance the investment
Joint Development	At-Grade Joint Development	Projects that occur within the existing development rights of a transportation project
	Above-Grade Joint Development	Projects that involve the transfer of air rights, which are development rights above or below transportation infrastructure
	Utility Joint Development	Projects that take advantage of the synergies of broadband and other utilities with highway right-of-way
Naming Rights	Naming Rights	A transaction that involves an agency selling the rights to name infrastructure to a private company

Source U.S. DOT (2019, p. 24)

Table 4.6 Value capture techniques and key features

Technique	Capital expenditure or O&M	Use for highways and roads	Funding or financing	Revenue Potential	Timing of revenue received	Ease of implementation	Public acceptance
Impact Fees	Capital Expenditure	Medium	Funding	Medium	Immediate	Simple	High
Negotiated Exactions	Capital Expenditure	Medium	Funding	Medium	Immediate	Simple	High
Transportation Utility Fees	O&M	High	Funding	Low	Delayed	Moderate	Medium
Special Assessment District	Capital Expenditure	Low	Funding & Financing	Medium/High	Delayed	Moderate	Medium
Business Improvement Districts	O&M/Capital Expenditures	Low	Funding	Low	Immediate	Moderate	High
Land Value Taxes	Capital Expenditure/O&M	Low	Funding	High	Delayed	Difficult	Low/Medium
Sales Tax Districts	Capital Expenditure	Medium	Funding & Financing	High	Delayed	Moderate	Medium
Tax Increment Financing	Capital Expenditure	Medium	Funding & Financing	Medium/High	Delayed	Moderate	Medium
Joint Development (including at-grade, above grade, and utility joint development)	Capital Expenditure	Medium	Funding & Financing	Medium	Immediate or delayed	Simple/Moderate	Medium
Naming Rights	Capital Expenditure/O&M	Medium	Funding	Low	Immediate	Simple	Medium/High

Source U.S. DOT (2019, p. 24)

cover total infrastructure capital costs, and (3) increased risk if the gains in property values are below forecast.

Examples: In 2003, the city of Lincoln, Nebraska, started its impact fee program. More than $34.3 million of impact fees have been collected to fund streets, water, sewer systems, and parks in the city's fastest growing areas.

The city of Kansas City, Missouri, created the Downtown Transportation Development District (DTDD) as the primary financial mechanism to fund the cost of a $102 million streetcar line. It collects a 1% sales tax on sales within the DTDD. The sales tax revenue is used to back $73.5 million in bonds. Special assessment fees are charged along the downtown streetcar line.

In Texas, TIF districts are also referred to as public improvement districts (PIDs) or tax increment reinvestment zones (TIRZs). The city of Houston created an Uptown TIRZ in 1999 to improve mobility in the area. In 2013, the city announced a plan to build a bus rapid transit (BRT) line on Post Oak Boulevard in Uptown Houston. The total cost of the new BRT line was projected at $177 million, with 46% of the cost paid for by Uptown TIRZ revenues.

4.3.6 New Fees: Resilience Fees

Description: In the U.S., natural disasters are occurring more frequently and are increasingly severe. With more than 50% of Americans living in coastal areas, key infrastructure sectors (e.g., highways, seaports, and energy facilities) are increasingly vulnerable to climate impacts such as rising sea levels, storm surges, and flooding. Inland local communities also face similar problems of wildfires, flooding, and drought. Currently, infrastructure for sustainability and resilience is an emerging issue that many state and local governments are beginning to address. Investing in sustainable and resilient infrastructure can prevent billions in future climate-related damages and economic losses. However, the need to build sustainable and climate-resilient infrastructure projects is straining the resources of many towns, cities, and counties.

Resilience fees are surcharges imposed on water and sewer usage or tax levies or surcharges on local property owners (Connecticut Governor's Council on Climate Change, 2020). Revenues collected from resilience fees are used to pay for sustainable and resilient infrastructure updates and initiatives. Usually, resilience fees based on water and sewer usage are more attractive than property taxes because many properties are exempt from property taxes, and there are more legal hurdles and political sensitivities to raising property taxes. Resilience fees could be calculated based on the degree of protection afforded, for example, by estimating the reduced risk of property damage. Resilience fees can be used to "recapture" the private benefits of reduced risk and lower insurance costs that flow from public investment in resilience (Connecticut Governor's Council on Climate Change, 2020).

Advantages and Disadvantages: The main advantages of resilience fees are that they: (1) provide revenue sources for adaptation and resilience funding, (2) save states and municipalities by avoided loss, and (3) reduce the need for borrowing. The primary disadvantages of resilience fees include that they: (1) may be complex and costly to administer, (2) directly increase bills, (3) their visibility can generate political opposition, and (4) might raise equity concerns for high-risk, low-income neighborhoods.

Example: There are few examples of levying resilience fees in the U.S. In Northampton, Massachusetts, the Stormwater and Flood Control Utility Ordinance was passed by the City Council on March 20, 2014, to establish the new Stormwater and Flood Control Utility and support integrated stormwater and resilience efforts. The new utility is supported by a resilience fee, which is a surcharge based on water and sewer usage.

4.4 New Financing Mechanisms

4.4.1 New Credit Assistance Tools: TIFIA Credit Assistance

Description: The Transportation Infrastructure Finance and Innovation Act of 1998 (TIFIA) provides federal credit assistance in the form of direct loans, loan guarantees, and standby lines of credit to finance surface transportation projects of national and regional significance (U.S. DOT, 2021a).

- Direct TIFIA loans are loans made to state and local project sponsors with low-interest rates and flexible repayment terms. TIFIA loans have a maximum term of 35 years. Loan repayments can start up to five years after the substantial completion of projects.
- Loan guarantees provide full-faith-and-credit guarantees by the federal government and guarantee a borrower's repayments to private lenders.
- Standby lines of credit represent a credit source of funding in the form of contingent federal loans that can be used to supplement project revenues.

The size of TIFIA loans cannot exceed 49% of the total eligible project cost. The amount of TIFIA loan guarantee and standby lines of credit is capped at 33% of the total eligible project cost. TIFIA interest rates are equivalent to Treasury rates. Depending on market conditions, TIFIA loan interest rates are often lower than what most borrowers can obtain in the private markets. Unlike private commercial loans with variable rate debt, TIFIA interest rates are fixed. Eligible projects can receive up to a $100 million loan. Table 4.7 describes TIFIA borrower and project eligibility.

According to U.S. DOT (2021a), as of 2021, TIFIA had financed 89 loan agreements totaling $35 billion (Table 4.8). The overall cost of the 89 projects supported by TIFIA loans is about $127 billion. The average project cost is $1.4 billion and the average loan amount $390 million. Consequently, the average TIFIA share of project costs has been about 27%. Among the 89 TIFIA loan agreements, 70 are active and 19 have been retired. Most of the projects have received a direct loan and, a majority of the projects are in the roads and bridges sector, followed by the public transit sector.

Advantages and Disadvantages: The main advantages of TIFIA credit assistance include: (1) lower interest rates, (2) flexible TIFIA repayment terms, (3) accelerating project construction, and (4) reduced total project cost. However, the significant disadvantages of TIFIA credit assistance are: (1) requirements to apply and compete for funding, (2) not applicable for small projects, (3) subject to the authorization of federal funding, and (4) compliance with all federal laws and regulations.

Table 4.7 TIFIA borrower and project eligibility

Borrower eligibility	Project eligibility
Public or publicly sponsored entity	"Shovel-ready" with all permits and licensing completed
Experienced with debt financing, such as prior TIFIA, Railroad Rehabilitation & Improvement Financing (RRIF)[a]	Investment grade rating from a nationally recognized agency
Willing to accept the terms of the standard TIFIA loan agreement template with little to no negotiation	Loan repayment source must be a general obligation pledge, dedicated tax revenue pledge, or government appropriations

[a]The Railroad Rehabilitation and Improvement Financing (RRIF) program was created by the U.S. Congress in 1998. It aims at offering low-cost and long-term loans to railroad operators (small freight railroads) and helping them finance improvements to railroad infrastructure and investments in equipment. Since 2000, the RRIF program has made 37 loans totaling $5.4 billion (valued at $5.9 billion in 2018 dollars) (U.S. Congressional Research Service, 2018)

Source U.S. DOT (2021b). https://www.transportation.gov/buildamerica/financing/tifia

Table 4.8 Value of TIFIA loans and total project costs by year closed

Fiscal year closed	Number of projects	TIFIA assistance (million dollar)	Total project cost (million dollar)	Share of TIFIA credit assistance in total project cost
FY1999	4	1,439	8,646	17%
FY2000	2	374	1,157	32%
FY2001	1	51	280	18%
FY2002	1	900	3,250	28%
FY2003	1	140	658	21%
FY2004	0	0	0	0%
FY2005	3	254	1,049	24%
FY2006	1	42	280	15%
FY2007	3	1,096	4,494	24%
FY2008	1	589	1,938	30%
FY2009	2	990	3,006	33%
FY2010	5	2,158	7,518	29%
FY2011	2	472	1,575	30%
FY2012	4	1,398	6,737	21%
FY2013	6	1,771	7,392	24%
FY2014	12	7,947	25,925	31%
FY2015	5	2,041	6,297	32%
FY2016	6	2,180	6,793	32%
FY2017	15	5,096	18,373	28%
FY2018	3	1,807	5,512	33%
FY2019	4	1,535	6,072	25%
FY2020	6	2,266	7,062	32%
FY2021	2	115	340	34%
Total	89	34,660	124,354	27%

Data Source U.S. Department of Transportation (2021a). Projects Financed by TIFIA. https://www.transportation.gov/buildamerica/projects/financing-search

Example: In 2012, the U.S. DOT awarded $545.9 million of TIFIA loans to Los Angeles County Metropolitan Transportation Authority to help build a new light rail transit line along the Crenshaw corridor. The total project cost is $1.75 billion. Revenue from a voter-approved local option sales tax was devoted to paying back the TIFIA loan.

4.4.2 Water Infrastructure Finance and Innovation Act (WIFIA)

Description: The WIFIA concept is modeled after the TIFIA program. The Water Infrastructure Finance and Innovation Act of 2014 established the

WIFIA program, a federal credit program administered by EPA for eligible water and wastewater infrastructure projects (Table 4.9). In general, the WIFIA program is designed to support larger infrastructure projects with eligible costs exceeding $20 million. Policymakers set a lower minimum

Table 4.9 WIFIA borrower and project eligibility

Borrower eligibility	Project eligibility	Activity eligibility
Local, state, tribal, and federal government entities	Projects that are eligible for the Clean Water SRF, notwithstanding the public ownership clause	Development phase activities, including planning, preliminary engineering, design, environmental review, revenue forecasting, and other pre-construction activities
Partnerships and joint ventures	Projects that are eligible for the Drinking Water SRF	Construction, reconstruction, rehabilitation, and replacement activities
Corporations and trusts	Enhanced energy efficiency projects at drinking water and wastewater facilities	Acquisition of real property or an interest in real property, environmental mitigation, construction contingencies, and acquisition of equipment
Clean Water and Drinking Water State Revolving Fund (SRF) programs	Brackish or seawater desalination, aquifer recharge, alternative water supply, and water recycling projects	Capitalized interest necessary to meet market requirements, reasonably required reserve funds, capital issuance expenses, and other carrying costs during construction
	Drought prevention, reduction, or mitigation projects	
	Acquisition of property if it is integral to the project or will mitigate the environmental impact of a project	
	A combination of projects secured by a common security pledge or submitted under one application by an SRF program	

Source U.S. EPA https://www.epa.gov/wifia/what-wifia

threshold for project costs ($5 million) for WIFIA projects in communities with populations less than 25,000. The maximum portion of eligible project costs that WIFIA can fund is 49%. The interest rate is equal or lower than the U.S. Treasury rate of similar maturity. This is typically lower than the rate at which state and local governments can borrow (Greer, 2020). In addition, total federal assistance may not exceed 80% of a project's eligible costs.

Figure 4.3 presents the financial model of WIFIA. As of 2021, WIFIA has closed 63 loans totaling $12.1 billion in credit assistance to help finance over $27 billion for water infrastructure projects and create 73,000 jobs (Table 4.10). The average project cost is $441 million and the average loan amount $193 million. Consequently, the average WIFIA share of project costs has been about 45%.

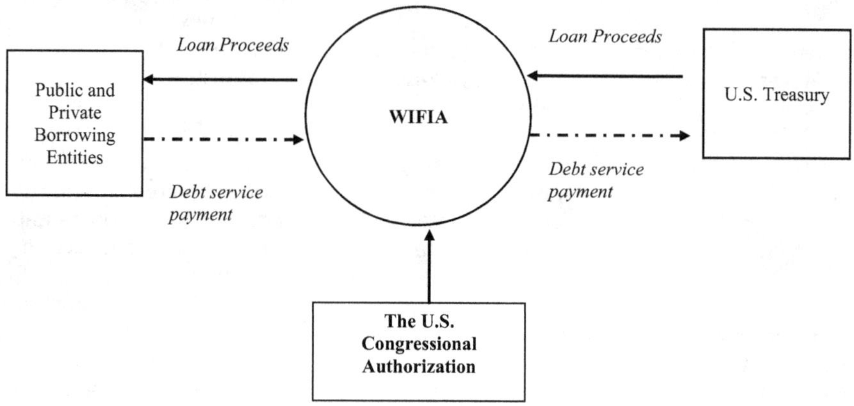

Fig. 4.3 Financial model for Water Infrastructure Finance and Innovation Act (WIFIA) (*Note* Private entities must have a public sponsor to be WIFIA-eligible. *Source* The Authors)

Table 4.10 Value of WIFIA loans and total project costs by year closed

Fiscal year closed	Number of projects	WIFIA assistance (million dollar)	Total project cost (million dollar)	Share of WIFIA credit assistance in total project cost
FY 2018	7	1,902	4,290	44%
FY 2019	7	1,681	3,776	45%
FY 2020	27	4,219	7,305	58%
FY 2021	22	4,364	12,424	35%
Total	63	12,165	27,795	45%

Data Source U.S. EPA (2021a). WIFIA Closed Loans. https://www.epa.gov/wifia/wifia-closed-loans

Advantages and Disadvantages: The main advantages of WIFIA credit assistance include: (1) a low and fixed interest rate, (2) flexible and customized loan repayment schedules, (3) accelerated project construction, and (4) it can be combined with private equity, revenue bonds, corporate debt, grants, and State Revolving Fund loans. The main disadvantages of WIFIA credit assistance include: (1) requirements to apply and compete for funding, (2) assistance is subject to the authorization of federal funding, and (3) required compliance with all federal laws and regulations.

Examples: On June 20, 2018, EPA issued a $69.7 million loan to the City of Omaha, Nebraska, to help finance its Saddle Creek Retention Treatment Basin. The project is part of the city's sewer system, serving 400,000 people over 300 square miles in the Omaha area. It is an important part of the $2 billion Clean Solutions Omaha plan required by the Nebraska Department of Environmental Quality to meet federal clean water requirements. This marks the second loan issued under the WIFIA program. The total project cost is $142.2 million. The use of the WIFIA loan saved the City of Omaha about $20 million in interest costs by utilizing WIFIA financing for this project (U.S. EPA, 2018).

4.4.3 Environmental State Revolving Funds (SRFs)

Description: SRFs are state-run entities capitalized by federal funds and state matching funds that offer loans with below-market interest rates to local jurisdictions. Loan repayments revolve back into the pool of funds to fund other local eligible projects (Chen, 2016a, 2016b). Currently, there are two types of environmental SRFs. Both are capitalized by EPA capitalization grants and require a minimum 20% match of state funds. The first type is Clean Water State Revolving Funds (CWSRFs), which provides low-cost loans to finance local eligible water quality projects. The CWSRF was created by the 1987 amendments to the Clean Water Act (CWA) as a financial assistance program for wastewater infrastructure projects. The following projects are eligible to receive CWSRF assistance:

- Construction of publicly owned treatment works
- Nonpoint source
- National estuary program project
- Decentralized wastewater treatment systems
- Stormwater

- Water conservation, efficiency, and reuse
- Watershed pilot projects
- Energy efficiency
- Water reuse
- Security measures at publicly owned treatment works
- Technical assistance

As of 2020, the CWSRFs program has provided approximately $145 billion of financial assistance by issuing 42,800 low-interest loans since its inception in 1988 (U.S. EPA, 2021b). The total cumulative value of federal CWSRF capitalization grants is $47 billion. The total cumulative state CWSRF contribution is $9 billion (Fig. 4.4). The cumulative federal return on investment is close to 300%. This means that for each $1 of federal CWSRF capitalization, $3 financial assistance has been provided to communities through the CWSRF program. The CWSRF loan rates are below market. For example, the weighted average CWSRF interest rate in 2020 was 1.2% (U.S. EPA, 2021b). In addition, small communities with population 10,000 or fewer have received about $33 billion CWSRF financial assistance (23% of the total CWSRF financial assistance).

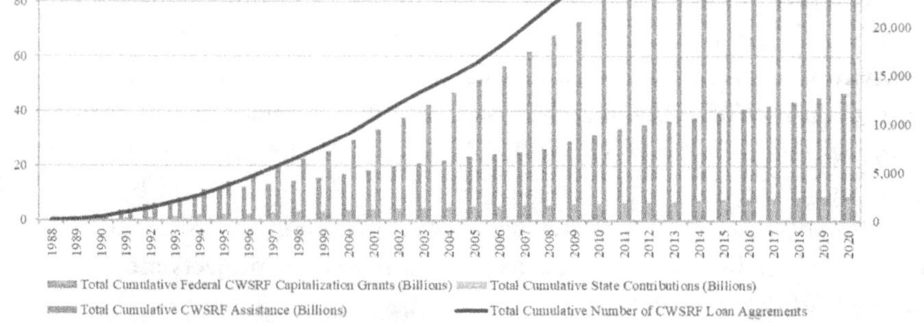

Fig. 4.4 CWSRF Program Assistance: 1988–2020 (*Data Source* U.S. EPA [2021b]. CWSRF National Information Management System Reports. https://www.epa.gov/cwsrf/clean-water-state-revolving-fund-cwsrf-national-information-management-system-reports)

Another environmental state revolving funds is the Drinking Water State Revolving Funds (DWSRFs) program to finance drinking water infrastructure improvements. The DWSRF was established by the 1996 amendments to the Safe Drinking Water Act (SDWA). It is a financial assistance program to help states and water systems to achieve the health protection objectives of the SDWA. The following projects are eligible to receive DWSRF assistance:

- Water Treatment
- Water Transmission and Distribution
- Water Source
- Water Storage
- Water Consolidation
- Water Creation of new systems

As of 2020, the DWSRFs program has entered into more than 16,300 assistance agreements and offered about $45 billion in low-interest loans to public water systems since its inception in 1997 (U.S. EPA, 2021c). The total cumulative value of federal DWSRF capitalization grants is $22 billion. The total cumulative state DWSRF contribution is $4 billion (Fig. 4.5). The cumulative federal return on investment is close to 207%. This infers that for

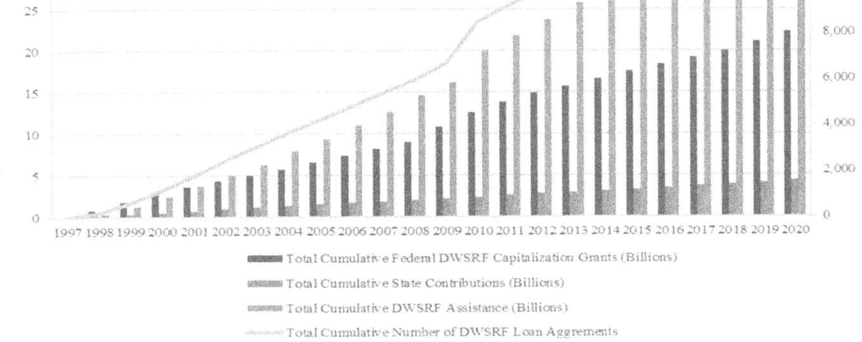

Fig. 4.5 DWSRF Program Assistance: 1997–2020 (*Data Source* U.S. EPA [2021b]. DWSRF National Information Management System Reports. https://www.epa.gov/dwsrf/drinking-water-state-revolving-fund-national-information-management-system-reports)

each $1 of federal DWSRF capitalization, $2 financial assistance has been provided to communities through the DWSRF program. The DWSRF loan rates are below market. For example, the weighted average DWSRF interest rate in 2020 was 1.3% (U.S. EPA, 2021c). In addition, over 30% of DWSRF assistance have been directed to communities with populations of 10,000 or fewer. Mullin and Daley (2018) investigate the stimulus effects of the Clean Water and the Drinking Water SRF Programs on local water infrastructure investment. Based on the analysis of 17 years of state-level panel data, they find that an additional dollar from the federal government into a state's loan fund translates into $2.84 in new spending on wastewater infrastructure. However, this significant stimulus effect was not evident in the Drinking Water SRF program, where federal dollars appear to displace existing spending rather than stimulate new investment.

Advantages and Disadvantages: The main advantages of SRFs include: (1) low-interest rate on loans, (2) flexible repayment terms, (3) stable and growing funding sources, and (4) ease of use by small communities. The main disadvantages of SRF include: (1) requirements to apply and compete for funding and (2) compliance with all federal and state laws and regulations.

Example: In 2015, the Georgia Environmental Finance Authority (GEFA) awarded CWSRF and DWSRF water infrastructure financing loans totaling $14 million to 11 Georgia cities and 2 local water authorities. These loans were used to help local communities build water, sewer, and wastewater infrastructure improvements.

4.4.4 State Infrastructure Banks (SIBs)

Description: Similar to the environmental SRFs, SIBs use seed capitalization funds from federal transportation aid and state-matching funds to get started and offer low-interest loans and non-grant forms of credit enhancements to public and private sponsors of state and local transportation projects. Loan repayments from existing project borrowers are recycled and available for future lending. As of 2015, SIBs have provided 972 low-interest loans to state and local governments with a total loan value of $5.8 billion (U.S. DOT, 2016b).

There are currently, three types of SIBs based on different sources of capitalization: federally capitalized, state-only capitalized, and hybrid (Puentes & Thompson, 2012). One type of SIB is the federally capitalized SIBs. There

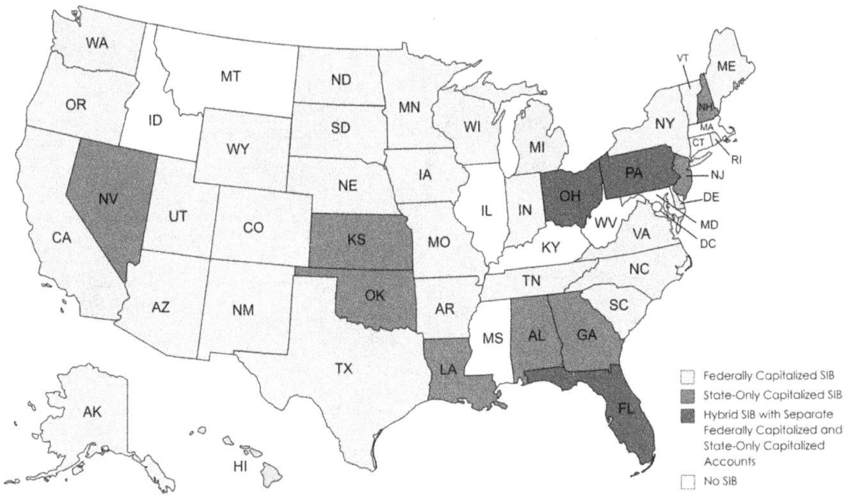

Fig. 4.6 State Infrastructure Banks (SIBs) by capitalized sources as of 2021 (*Data Source* BATIC Institute [2021] and U.S. FHWA Center for Innovative Finance Support [2021])

are 33 federally capitalized SIBs that use a blend of federal and state capitalized funds to finance federally authorized projects (see Fig. 4.6). State-only capitalized SIBs exclusively utilize state funds to leverage other forms of capital investment to fund a broader range of state and local projects. The typical examples are the Kansas Transportation Revolving Fund and the Georgia Transportation Infrastructure Bank. Recently, four states have enacted enabling legislations to create state-only capitalized SIBs: Louisiana and New Hampshire (2014), Alabama (2015), New Jersey (2016), and Nevada (2017).[2]

The hybrid SIB operates with separate federally capitalized and state-only capitalized accounts (Ohio, Florida, Pennsylvania, and Virginia). SIBs with state-only capitalized fund accounts have more flexibility in funding state and local transportation projects because they do not need to comply with federal rules and requirements under Titles 23 and 49.

Figure 4.7 illustrates the financial operation of federally capitalized SIBs. A SIB uses seed capitalization funds from federal transportation aid and state-matching funds to get started and offers low-interest loans and credit enhancements in the forms of loan guarantees, letters of credit, and lines of credit to eligible state and local transportation projects. The key feature

[2] In 2017, Nevada state lawmakers approved legislation creating the structure and function of the State Infrastructure Bank. However, the state has never allocated any funding for this bank. In 2021, Nevada Governor Steve Sisolak pushes efforts to fund a state infrastructure bank.

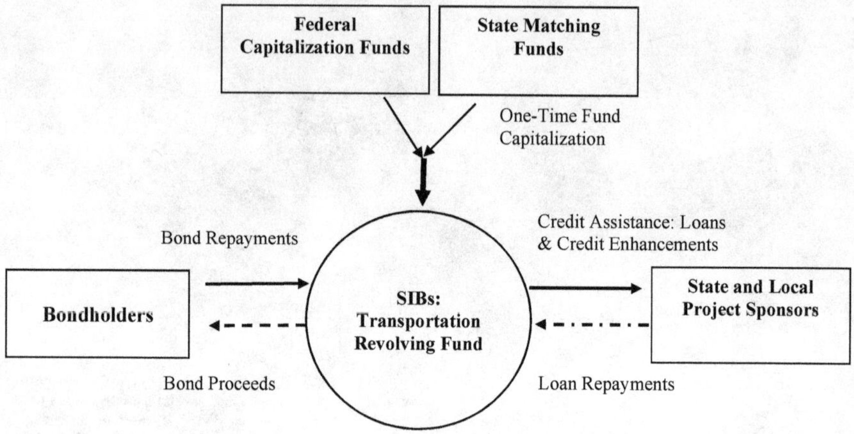

Fig. 4.7 Financial model for federally capitalized State Infrastructure Banks (SIBs) (*Source* The Authors)

of SIBs is offering subsidized loans to transportation projects rather than traditional grants. Initial SIB loan repayments are recycled and revolved for second round projects, furthering the capacity to assist more transportation projects. In addition, localities receiving credit enhancements from SIBs benefit from lower interest rates, improved marketability of bonds, and lower project financing costs. A SIB can opt to expand initial capitalization by issuing bonds, and then use the bond proceeds to assist more or larger transportation projects. Bonds are secured by state and local project sponsors' loan repayments.

SIBs can provide different kinds of financial assistance to project sponsors, from low-interest rate loans to credit support. The majority of SIB loan recipients benefited from lower borrowing costs compared with alternative municipal bond financing (Yusuf et al., 2010). In addition, SIBs leverage their initial equity funds to increase state and local transportation investments. Chen (2016b) finds that for every dollar of SIB loan disbursement to state and local highway project sponsors, state and local highway capital expenditure increased by nearly three dollars on average over a three-year period.

Finally, by lowering financial risk, SIBs can help attract private developers wishing to take an equity interest in transportation projects. For example, the Pennsylvania Infrastructure Bank has made many loans to local transportation projects involving private partners. However, in practice, SIBs vary widely across states in terms of program implementation. The Great Recession hurt states' capacities to provide new infusions of capital to existing SIBs.

For example, since 2009, the Arizona SIB (Highway Expansion and Extension Loan Program) has stopped making new loans to localities due to the need to repay its debt obligations.

State Infrastructure Bank Best Practices

In the 2017 State Infrastructure Bank (SIB) Peer Exchange, the U.S. Federal Highway Administration (2017) identifies the following best practices and lessons of operating the SIB program:

- **Targeted Marketing**. A series of SIB outreach and promotional activities are directed to a wide array of state and local government agencies, (e.g., state transportation agencies, counties, municipalities, turnpike authorities), professional associations (as an association of counties, and a league of municipalities), as well as state and local government financial advisors and consultants. For instance, the Texas SIB regularly promotes its SIB program to engineering and planning personnel at each of TxDOT's 25 districts.
- **Application Process**. Establishing a transparent, easy to understand, easy to access, and regular application process (on a quarterly or annual basis) is important to attract a large number of potential borrowers. Moreover, developing formal loan application templates, loan evaluation and selection criteria, and forming loan selection committees are valuable.
- **Loan Features**. Loan features (terms and payment structures,) are tailored to reflect the needs of the projects. SIB loan interest rates are set at or below market to ensure SIB credit assistances are attractive.
- **Prudent Leveraging**. Prudent leveraging of SIB programs (issuing bonds) can increase the deposit capital available for lending. Both the Florida and Ohio SIBs have issued bonds using deposit capital as collateral.
- **Program Management**. Imposing borrowing limits (a minimum borrowing among requirement and a maximum borrowing amount limits) for projects and borrowers.

Source U.S. DOT. (2017). *State Infrastructure Bank Best Practices*. https://www.fhwa.dot.gov/ipd/pdfs/finance/sib_best_practices_1117.pdf.

Advantages and Disadvantages: The main advantages of SIBs include: (1) lower interest rates, (2) flexible loan repayment terms, (3) accelerating project construction, and (4) attracting private partners. The main disadvantages of SIB include: (1) many SIBs are inactive and underutilized, (2) requirements to apply and compete for funding, and (3) compliance with all federal and state laws and regulations.

Examples: The Ohio State Infrastructure Bank (Ohio SIB) is one of the most active and successful state infrastructure banks in the nation. In 2020, the Ohio SIB awarded 7 loans totaling $15.2 million to local communities for a wide array of transportation projects. Since its inception of the program in 1995, the Ohio SIB has issued 252 loans and 12 bonds for a total of $768.7 million (Ohio SIB, Ohio Department of Transportation 2021).

In 2013, Dauphin County, Pennsylvania, established the first-ever county-level infrastructure bank to make low-interest loans to municipalities and private developers for transportation improvements. In 2014, this bank awarded $3.9 million in low-interest loans to five local infrastructure projects.

4.4.5 New Bonds and Debt Financing Tools: GARVEEs

Description: According to U.S. DOT (2016c), Grant Anticipation Revenue Vehicle Bonds (GARVEEs) are bonds or notes issued by states and local governments with the pledge of anticipated future federal-aid highway grants (Fig. 4.8). The issuance of GARVEEs enables state and local governments to obtain up-front financing and accelerate highway construction. It also leverages federal funds and increases state borrowing capacity. It should be noted that GARVEEs are the debt obligation of state and local governments rather than federal obligations. Because GARVEEs are subject to federal funding authorization, they generally have more risk than general municipal bonds.

Generally, the eligible projects for GARVEE financing have the following characteristics (U.S. DOT, 2021b):

- The project size is large enough to merit borrowing rather than pay-go grant funding. Besides GARVEE, other borrowing options are not feasible.
- There is no dedicated revenue sources (local taxes or tolls) and state funding options for the project.

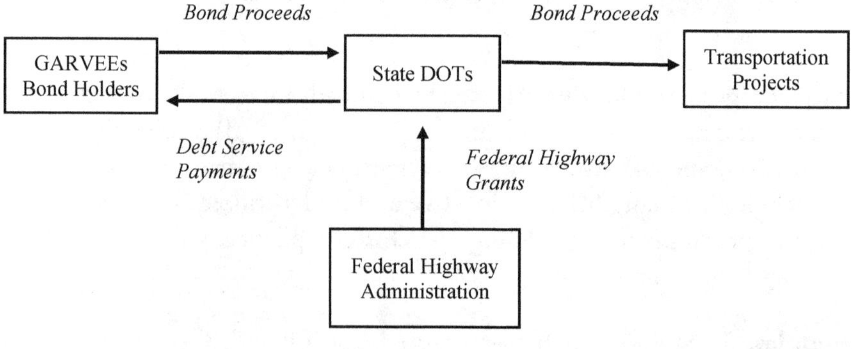

Fig. 4.8 Financial model for Grant Anticipation Revenue Vehicle Bonds (GARVEEs) (*Source* The Authors)

- The project sponsors (generally state DOTs) are willing to reserve a portion of anticipated Federal-aid highway funds in future to satisfy current debt service requirements.

Table 4.11 and Fig. 4.9 show that as of October 2021, 27 have issued more than $25 billion in GARVEEs (U.S. DOT, 2021b). Ohio has the largest amount of GARVEE bond issues ($2.7 billion), accounting for more than 10% of total state GARVEE bond issues. Colorado and Georgia are ranked 2nd and 3rd, respectively. They have issued $2.3 billion and $2.1 billion GARVEE bond issues, respectively.

Table 4.11 GARVEE Bond issues by states as of October 2021

Sate	GARVEE Bond issues (millions)	Share in total GARVEE Bond issues
Alabama	1,709	6.8%
Alaska	103	0.4%
Arizona	1,028	4.1%
Arkansas	1,403	5.6%
California	713	2.8%
Colorado	2,290	9.1%
Delaware	308	1.2%
Georgia	2,087	8.3%
Idaho	1,366	5.4%
Kentucky	999	4.0%
Louisiana	340	1.4%
Maine	353	1.4%
Maryland	817	3.2%
Mississippi	1,479	5.9%
Montana	241	1.0%
New Hampshire	178	0.7%
New Jersey	132	0.5%
New Mexico	353	1.4%
North Carolina	1,945	7.7%
North Dakota	51	0.2%
Ohio	2,737	10.9%
Oklahoma	352	1.4%
Rhode Island	1,213	4.8%
Virginia	1,669	6.6%
Washington	786	3.1%
West Virginia	538	2.1%
Total	25,189	100.0%

Data Source U.S. DOT (2021b). Current GARVEE activity. https://www.fhwa.dot.gov/ipd/finance/tools_programs/federal_debt_financing/garvees/garvee_state_by_state.aspx

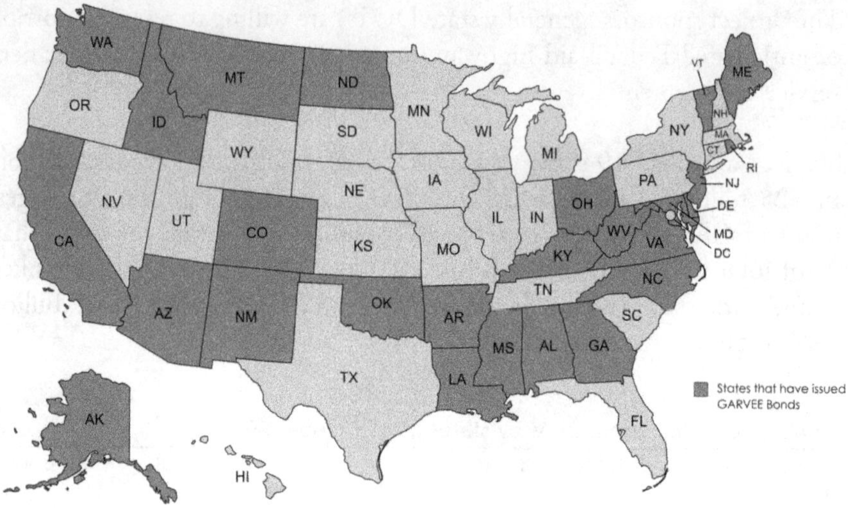

Fig. 4.9 Map of GARVEE Bond issues by states as of October 2021 (*Data Source* U.S. DOT [2021b]. Current GARVEE activity. https://www.fhwa.dot.gov/ipd/finance/tools_programs/federal_debt_financing/garvees/garvee_state_by_state.aspx)

Advantages and Disadvantages: The main advantages of GARVEEs include the ability to: (1) quickly obtaining up-front financing sources, (2) accelerate project construction, and (3) leverage large amounts of financing. The main disadvantage of GARVEEs include: (1) they lay claim on anticipated future federal funds, (2) they are subject to the authorization of federal funding, and (3) they require compliance with all federal laws and regulations.

Example: In 2005, the California Transit Finance Authority issued a $25,475,000 GARVEE revenue bond on behalf of the Ventura County Transportation Commission to finance the Lewis Road widening project in Ventura County. In 2016, the Georgia State Transportation Board (the policy-making body of the Georgia Department of Transportation) and the Board of Directors of the State Road and Tollway Authority (SRTA) have approved the sale of GARVEE bonds to fund early purchase of needed right-of-way on the Revive 285 projects (12 miles of two new express lanes along both sides of I-285 from I-75 in Cobb County to I-85 in DeKalb County). GARVEE bonds are secured primarily with future federal transportation funds.

4.4.6 Green Bonds

Description: In general, green bonds are regular bonds but issued to exclusively finance or refinance new and/or existing eligible "green" projects that have significant environmental benefits such as renewable energy, energy efficiency, sustainable waste management, sustainable forestry and land use, and other projects that mitigate climate change. Issuers agree to the disclosures required by the Green Bond Principles (GBP) of the International Capital Market Association.

Four Types of Green Bonds in the Capital Market

- **Standard Green Use of Proceeds Bond**: These green bonds are secured by green assets comparable to those of standard bonds. The bond proceeds are held in a sub-portfolio or otherwise tracked by the issuer and attested to by a formal internal process that is linked to the issuer's lending and investment operations for projects.
- **Green Revenue Bond**: Use of proceeds revenue bonds are secured by income-generating projects (the pledged cash flows of the revenue streams, fees, taxes, etc.) and whose use of proceeds go to related or unrelated green projects.
- **Green Project Bond**: A project bond for a single or multiple green projects aligned with the GBP for which the investor has direct exposure to the risk of the project(s) with or without potential recourse to the bond issuer.
- **Green Securitized Bond**: A bond collateralized by one or multiple green projects aligned with GBP. It can include mortgage-backed securities (MBS), asset-backed securities (ABS), or others. (MBS are bonds secured by real estate loans. ABS means financial securities backed by income-generating assets such as student loans and credit card receivables)

Source International Capital Market Association (2021). *The green bond principles (GBP) 2021*. https://www.icmagroup.org/sustainable-finance/the-principles-guidelines-and-handbooks/green-bond-principles-gbp/.

The latest updated 2021 Green Bond Principles provide broad categories for suitable green activities (International Capital Market Association, 2021, pp. 4–5):

- Renewable energy,
- Energy efficiency,
- Pollution prevention and control,
- Environmentally sustainable management of living natural resources and land use,

- Terrestrial and aquatic biodiversity conservation,
- Clean transportation,
- Sustainable water and wastewater management,
- Climate change adaption,
- Circular economy adapted products, production technologies and processes; and/or certified eco-efficient products,
- Green buildings.

Figure 4.10 presents the financial model of green bonds. The first Climate Awareness Green Bond was issued by the European Investment Bank in 2007. Since then, the green bond market has been expanding rapidly. In the U.S., Massachusetts issued the first tax-exempt municipal green bond of $99 million in 2017 for environmental projects (see Sect. 5.3.4). The green bond market has grown rapidly in recent years. According to data compiled by the Climate Bond Initiative (CBI), in 2020, $269.5 billion were issued worldwide. In the U.S., municipal green bond issuances grew by 450% from roughly $2.9 billion in 2014 to almost $12.5 billion in 2017. The number and value of green bonds issued by municipalities plummeted in 2018 (see Fig. 4.11) but recovered to higher levels in 2019. In 2020, the value of municipal green bond issue was 20.4 billion, accounting for 4% of total U.S. municipal bond issuances.

Advantages and Disadvantages: The main advantages of green bonds include: (1) attracting new capital market investors interested in environmental projects, (2) improving bond issuers' environmental performance, and (3) enhancing bond issuers' reputation for environmental sustainability. The main disadvantages of green bonds include: (1) additional monitoring and

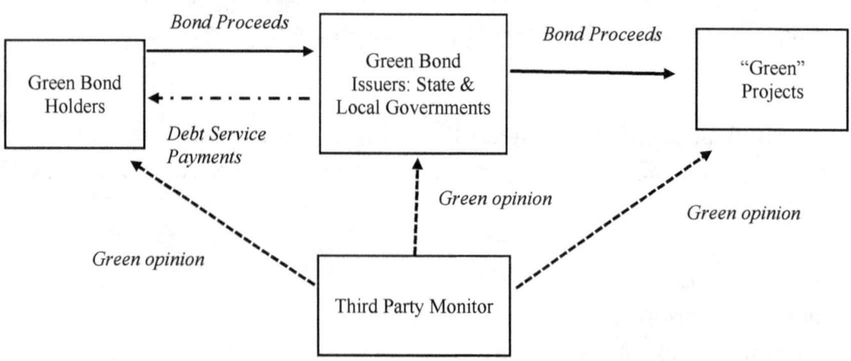

Fig. 4.10 Financial model for Green Bonds (*Source* The Authors)

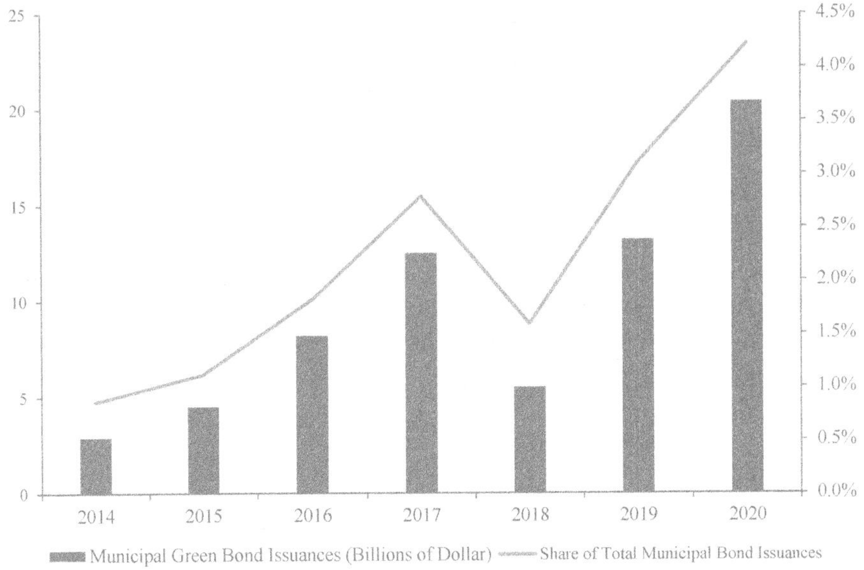

Fig. 4.11 Growth of municipal Green Bond issues: 2014–2020 (*Data Source* Bloomberg. https://www.bloomberg.com/news/articles/2021-04-20/biden-spending-plan-seen-jolting-muni-green-bond-sales-to-record)

reporting green projects and (2) a less developed market than traditional municipal bonds.

Example: The New York Metropolitan Transport Authority (MTA) provides a mass transport system for the New York metropolitan area. It is the largest regional public transportation provider in the Western Hemisphere, serving approximately 14.6 million people spread over 5,000 square miles (13,000 km^2) in New York State and Connecticut. This includes commuter rail routes, subway routes, rapid transit, and bus routes. In 2016, New York's MTA issued $500 million in Transportation Revenue Green Bonds for infrastructure renewal and upgraded projects for New York City transit. Proceeds from bond sales were allocated for capital investments in MTA's electrified rail assets and supporting infrastructure.

4.4.7 Social Impact Bonds

Description: Social impact bonds, also known as pay-for-success financing, pay-for-success bond, social benefit bond, or simply a social bond, are an innovative performance or outcome-based financing tool that enables governments to pay for programs that meet the expected social outcomes (Harvard Kennedy School, 2013). Despite their name, SIBs are not municipal bonds with a fixed rate of return. Instead, they are a financing instrument in which repayment of principal and a rate of return is contingent on the success of achieving agreed-upon program goals (see Fig. 4.12).

For instance, in New York City, the goal of one social impact bond program is to reduce recidivism among incarcerated adolescents by 8% and to increase employment by 5%. Investors will be repaid if these outcomes are achieved; however, investors stand to lose all but 10% of their investment if the outcomes are not achieved (The City of New York, 2012). In this sense, SIBs are a debt financing tool that pays for success. In most cases, SIBs are used to finance social infrastructure projects such as hospitals, prisons, and affordable housing.

The first SIB was issued in the United Kingdom in 2010, followed by 14 others in the U.K. and the U.S. in 2012. According to the Brookings Global Impact Bonds Database, as of November 1, 2021, 219 social impact bonds have been implemented in 33 countries across six sectors (social welfare, employment, health, education, criminal justice, environment & agriculture), raising a total amount of more than $458 million in total outcome funding committed (Gustasson-Wright, 2020). Over 2 million beneficiaries have been targeted to receive services. As Fig. 4.13 demonstrates, there is considerable variation in the number of impact bond beneficiaries. India, the U.S., and Portugal are the top three countries in terms of the number of impact bond

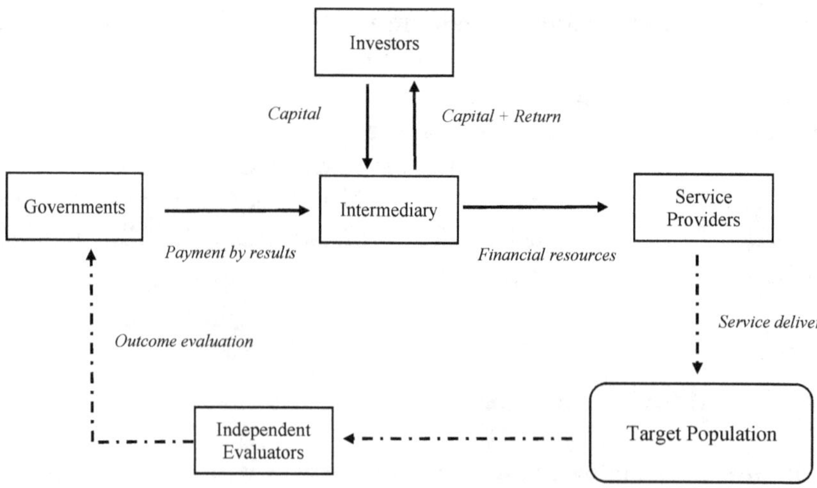

Fig. 4.12 The financial model for social impact bonds (*Source* The Authors)

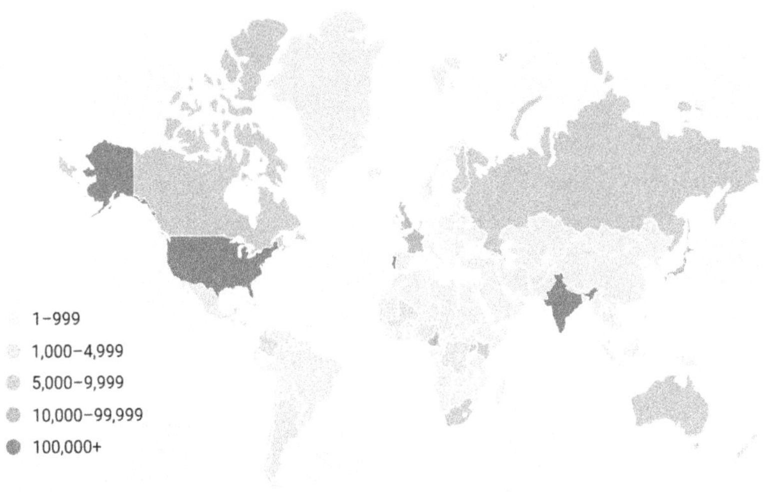

Fig. 4.13 The beneficiaries of social impact bonds by country (*Data Source* Brookings Global Impact Bonds Database. https://www.brookings.edu/research/social-and-development-impact-bonds-by-the-numbers/)

beneficiaries. The majority of beneficiaries are young children, disadvantaged young people due to unemployment or other social issues, and individuals experiencing homelessness (Gustasson-Wright, 2020).

Advantages and Disadvantages: The main advantages of SIBs include: (1) attracting new investors from nonprofit organizations, philanthropic foundations, and corporations and (2) transferring government risks to the private and nonprofit sectors. The main disadvantages of SIBs include: (1) they are largely in the experimental phase, (2) they may have a complicated contract process, and (3) the risky nature of social programs.

Examples: In 2012, New York City issued the first social impact bond of \$9.6 million for a prisoner rehabilitation program to reduce teen recidivism among adolescents incarcerated on Rikers Island. As indicated in Fig. 4.14, in partnership with the City of New Work, Goldman Sachs and Bloomberg Philanthropies are the private investors. Goldman Sachs provides a \$9.6 million loan through its Urban Investment Group. Bloomberg Philanthropies offered a \$7.2 million grant to guarantee a portion of the loan (loan guarantee). The intermediary is the Manpower Demonstration Research Corporation (MDRC). MDRC is a nonprofit and nonpartisan education and social policy research organization. As the intermediary, the main responsibilities of MDRC include setting up the financial arrangements, choosing the intervention and the service provider, training staff, and monitoring program

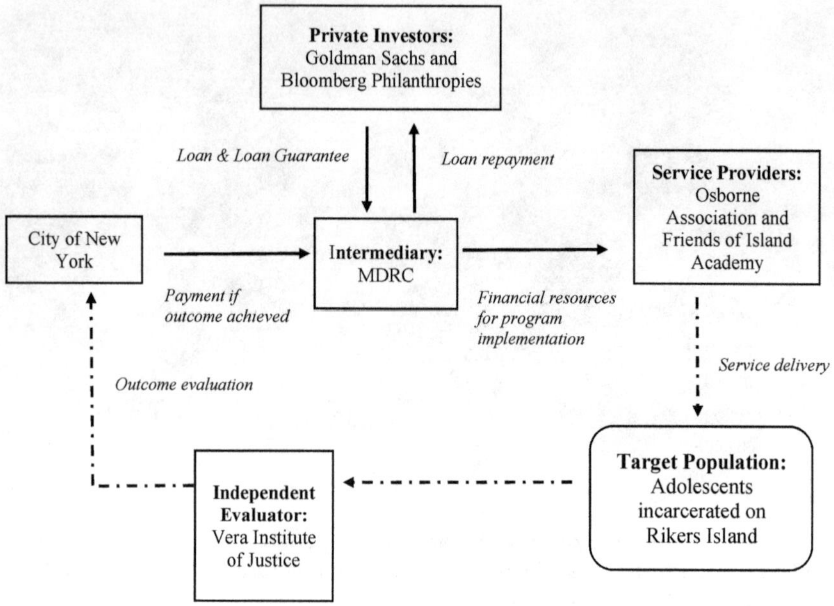

Fig. 4.14 The financial model of first U.S. social impact bond financed (*Source* The Authors)

communication and implementation. The two nonprofit organizations—Osborne Association and Friends of Island Academy are selected as the service providers who deliver the intervention to 16- to 18-year-old youth detained at Rikers Island. The Vera Institute of Justice serves as the independent evaluator and conducts a quasi-experimental valuation of the intervention. The City of New Work promised to pay MDRC based on the rate of reduced recidivism (Table 4.12). If recidivism goals are met or exceeded, the City of New Work pays $9.6 million to MDRC plus a return based on performance. If recidivism goals are not met, MDRC uses Bloomberg Philanthropies' $7.2 million to repay Goldman Sachs.

In 2015 July, the Vera Institute concluded that the intervention had failed to reduce recidivism. Consequently, the program ended in August 2015 (Berlin, 2016). Although the first U.S. social impact bond failed to produce the desired results, it attracted private capital to reduce juvenile recidivism and shifted the risk of program cost from the public sector to private investors.

Table 4.12 Payment terms for first U.S. social impact bond financed by Goldman Sachs

Two-year recidivism reduction rate	NYC department of correction success payment ($)	Net projected taxpayer savings ($)
≥20.0%	11,712,000	20,500,000
≥16.0%	10,944,000	11,700,000
≥13.0%	10,368,000	7,200,000
≥12.5%	10,272,000	6,400,000
≥12.0%	10,176,000	5,600,000
≥11.0%	10,080,000	1,700,000
≥10.0%	9,600,000	<1,000,000
≥8.5%	4,800,000	<1,000,000

Source Rudd et al. (2013)

4.4.8 Environmental Impact Bonds

Description: Modeled after the Social Impact Bonds, Environmental Impact Bonds (EIBs) are an innovative performance-based financing tool that provides up-front capital from private investors for environmental projects (Quantified Ventures, 2018). Similar to a typical municipal bond, EIBs offer up-front private capital to pay for environmental projects. However, unlike municipal bonds, EIBs use a pay-for-success approach that conditions payback to investors based on the performance of environmental projects. In its most basic model (Fig. 4.15), private investors participate in the pay-for-success approach and provide up-front capital through bond investments to implement environmental projects. Following project construction and evaluation, the payor, the public agency, repays private investors based on the achievement of agreed-upon project outcomes (Quantified Ventures, 2018).

In the U.S., the first EIB was issued Washington D.C. Water in 2016 to finance the construction of green infrastructure to manage stormwater. Since then, the impact investment firm—Quantified Ventures has structured EIBs with many other municipalities and utilities. In 2019, the City of Atlanta, Georgia, in partnership with Quantified Ventures issued the second U.S. EIB with the amount of $14 million. The Atlanta EIB provides funding for innovative green infrastructure projects that will address critical flooding and water quality issues and reduce stormwater runoff in Proctor Creek watershed. The Atlanta EIB issuance was supported by a grant from the Rockefeller Foundation with additional underwriting support offered by KeyBanc Capital Markets and Siebert Cisneros Shank. In 2020, the City of Hampton,

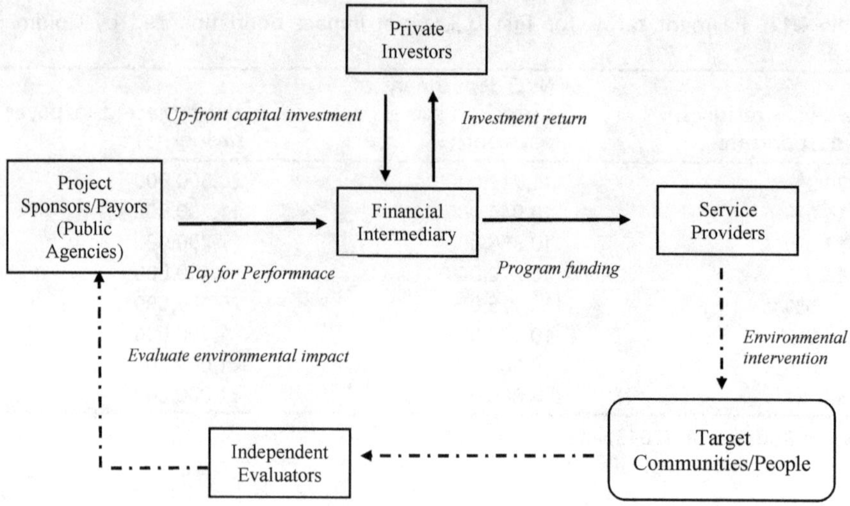

Fig. 4.15 The financial model of Environmental Impact Bonds (EIBs) (*Source* The Authors)

Virginia became the third U.S. community to issue an EIB to construct three major green infrastructure projects valued at about $12 million.

Advantages and Disadvantages: The main advantages of EIBs include: (1) risk transfer from public sectors to private and nonprofit sectors, (2) harnessing capital, expertise, and reputation from private and nonprofit organizations, (3) harnessing philanthropic and pro-social motivations among investors, and (4) emphasis on long-term outcomes. The main disadvantages of EIBs are: (1) the complexity of bond structure, (2) high transaction costs, and (3) it may be hard to measure the long-term outcomes.

Example: As part of its green infrastructure investment strategy, in 2016, Washington D.C. Water (EPA and the District of Columbia Water and Sewer Authority) issued a $25 million Environmental Impact Bond (EIB) to finance the construction of green infrastructure to manage stormwater runoff. The D.C. Water Bond was the first issued EIB in the U.S. It was issued by project developers, Quantified Ventures. This bond was not publicly issued; instead, it was privately sold to the investors (Goldman Sachs and Calvert Impact Capital) who bore the financial risk of EIB. The paying beneficiary was the D.C. Water agency and the consumers of water in the D.C. area. The bond is structured in the format of pay-for-performance with the key performance metric: the volume of stormwater reduction. The key interest rate was initially set at 3.43% for 30 years with a mixed environmental benefit repayment structure with a pay-for-performance component (Table 4.13).

Table 4.13 The DC Water EIB contingent payment structure

Performance tier	Outcome ranges	Contingent payment
1	Stormwater Runoff Reduction > 41.3%	DC Water will make an Outcome Payment to Investors of $3.3 million
2	18.6% <= Runoff Reduction <= 41.3%	No contingent payment due
3	Stormwater Runoff Reduction < 18.6%	Investors will make Risk Share Payment to DC Water of $3.3 million

Source The Washington D.C. Water (No Date)

Performance tier 1 reflects over-performance (the stormwater runoff reduction is greater than 41.3%). D.C. Water would have made an additional outcome payment to the investors for sharing its risk in the project. Performance tier 2 meets the expectation of the stormwater runoff reduction that resulted in no contingent payment due by either party. Performance tier 3 indicated under-performing expectations, and the stormwater runoff reduction was less than 18.6%. Therefore, the investors would have made a Risk Share Payment to D.C. Water. In 2020, D.C. Water announced the success of its innovative EIB. The green infrastructure projects financed by the D.C. EIB reduced stormwater runoff by nearly 20 percent from previous levels and achieved the performance goals set in 2016 (Performance tier 2).

4.4.9 Catastrophe Bonds and Resilience Bonds

Description: Given the growing impact of climate change, governments have begun to use catastrophe bonds and resilience bonds to transfer risks from the public sector to the capital market.[3] Catastrophe bonds (cat bonds) are more like insurance policies than traditional municipal bonds. They are issued to reduce the financial risks associated with very low-probability and high-consequence natural disasters (Vajjhala and Rhodes, 2018, p. 60). The unique feature of catastrophe bonds is that when a disaster reaches a predetermined threshold (e.g., $10 billion in losses) during the bond term (typically 3–5 years), the catastrophe bond policyholder retains the full value of the bond to pay off disaster losses, and investors lose part or all of their

[3] It should be noted that both catastrophe bonds and resilience bonds are insurance products. They are not typical municipal bonds. Public sector sponsors are only responsible for paying premiums, not for repaying bond principal. This helps state and local governments avoid the concern of approaching their debt limit or affecting their credit ratings.

invested principal. Catastrophe bond issuance in 2020 reached a record-high, as the market saw over $11 billion of pure property cat bonds issued for the first time.

Resilience bonds are a variation on catastrophe bonds that link insurance premiums to resilience projects to monetize avoided losses (e.g., reduction of hurricane insurance costs and claim) via a rebate structure (Vajjhala & Rhodes, 2018, p. 60). The key difference between catastrophe bonds (Fig. 4.16) and resilience bonds (Fig. 4.17) is that resilience bonds explicitly incorporate the risk reduction value of a specific resilience project on the expected loss to investors. Because the construction of a resilient infrastructure project can reduce the risk to investors (risk of losing their invested principal), this leads to lower premium payments for public sector sponsors. With resilience bonds, the residence rebate (the cost savings from the reduced coupon payments to investors) is distributed to public sector sponsors.

Advantages and Disadvantages: The main advantages of catastrophe bonds and resilience bonds include: (1) they are appealing to private investors, (2) they transfer risk from the public sector to capital markets, (3) they leverage private investment in resilient infrastructure, and (4) they may be more affordable than insurance for public sector sponsors. The main disadvantages of catastrophe bonds and resilience bonds are: (1) the complexity of the bond structure and (2) the high transaction costs.

Examples: The New York Metropolitan Transit Authority (MTA) experienced significant subway flooding during Hurricane Sandy in 2012. MTA

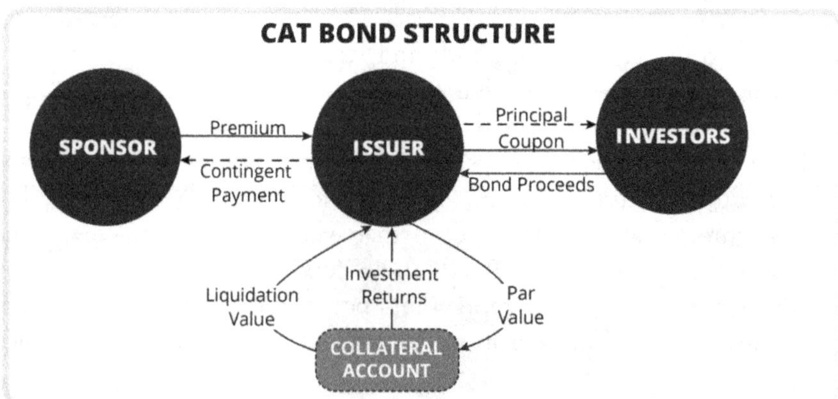

Fig. 4.16 Catastrophe bond structure (*Source* Refocuspartners.com [2017]. https://www.refocuspartners.com/wp-content/uploads/pdf/RE.bound-Program-Report-September-2017.pdf. Permission Granted)

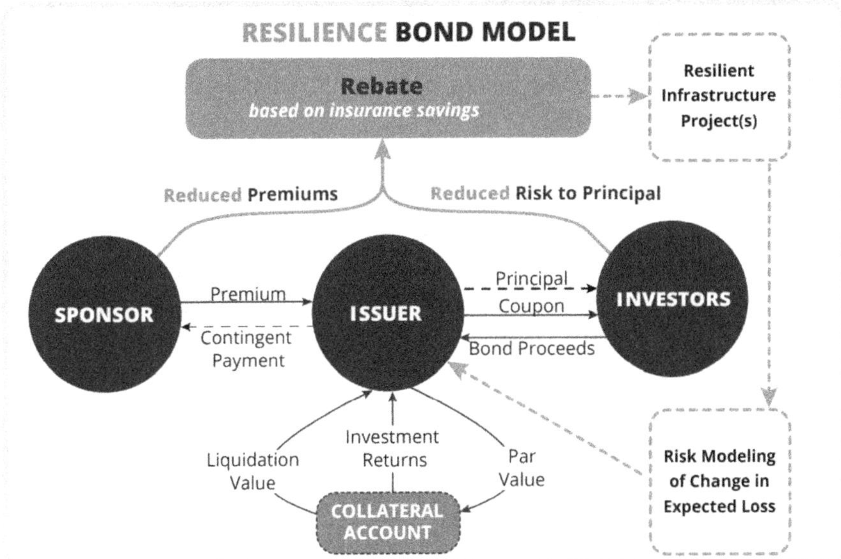

Fig. 4.17 Resilience Bond Model (*Source* Refocuspartners.com [2017]. https://www.refocuspartners.com/wp-content/uploads/pdf/RE.bound-Program-Report-September-2017.pdf)

Chairman and CEO Thomas F. Prendergast noted, "In the aftermath of Superstorm Sandy, the traditional avenues we use for insurance and reinsurance contracted dramatically, making it exceedingly difficult for the MTA to obtain insurance" (Hemenway, 2013). The MTA secured $200 million in coverage through a catastrophe bond at premium costs well below quotes received from traditional property coverage. It also enables shifting extreme risk to private insurers and investors in the capital market. To date, resilience bonds are currently in the concept stage. There are no use of resilience bonds in the U.S. However, with the growing interests in climate resilience and environmental sustainability, there could be a place for resilience bonds in future.

4.5 New Financial Arrangements

4.5.1 New Financial Arrangements: Public–Private Partnerships (P3s)

Description: P3s are contractual arrangements in which governments form partnerships with the private sector to design, finance, build, and operate and/or maintain infrastructures such as toll roads, water supply facilities, and wastewater treatment plants (U.S. DOT, 2012). Many different types of P3s (Fig. 4.18) exist because each of the five elements of development (design, finance, build, operate, and maintain) can be combined. For instance,

- In the design-build (DB) arrangement, a government agency establishes a fixed-fee contract with a private company that assumes the design and construction phases of the transportation infrastructure projects.
- In the design-build-operate-maintain (DBOM) arrangement, contracted private entities are responsible for project design and construction and take responsibility for the operation and maintenance of transportation projects. Public agencies oversee financing and assume all the risks related to operating costs and project revenues.
- In the design-build-finance-operate-maintain (DBFOM) arrangement, private entities also take the responsibility of fully or partially funding transportation projects. Revenue generated from transportation projects (tolls or fares) is used to pay for the project costs. Public agencies still retain the ownership of privately built transportation projects.

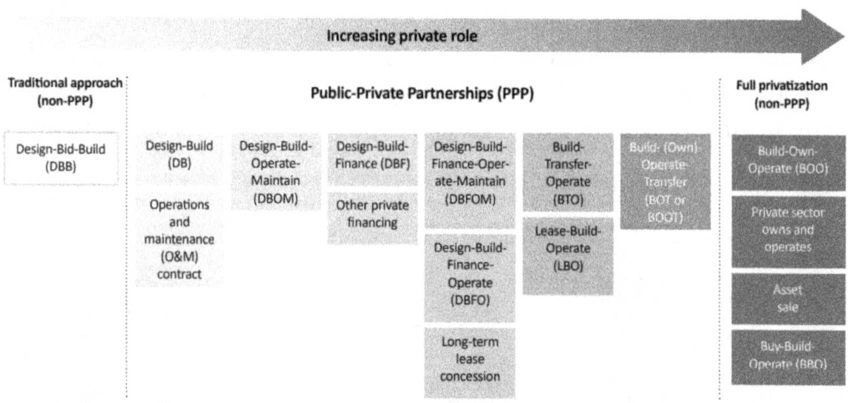

Fig. 4.18 Private role in infrastructure delivery (*Source* NCSL [2017]. P3 infrastructure delivery: principles for state legislature. https://www.ncsl.org/Portals/1/documents/transportation/P3_Infrastructure_080117.pdf. Permission Granted)

- The last type of P3s is a concession, which means a private entity makes an up-front payment and agrees to operate, maintain, or improve public assets during the term of the lease (Table 4.14).

From 1996 to 2016, there were 221 P3 projects. As indicated in Table 4.15, the majority of these P3 projects are Design-Build (53.9%). About 32% of P3s projects have a financing component. 14.5% of involve operations or maintenance without a financing component. As indicated in Fig. 4.19, as of August 2018, 36 states had authorized P3-enabling legislation with varying degrees of favorability for transportation projects (U.S. DOT, 2018). State

Table 4.14 Types of P3s

P3 type	Characteristics
Design-Build (DB)	Design (D) and construction (B) are bundled into one procurement and contract
Design-Build-Finance (DBF)	Design (D) and construction (B) are bundled into one procurement and contract with financing (F) provided by the contractor
Design-Build-Maintain (DBM)	Design (D), construction (B), and maintenance (M) are bundled into one procurement and contract
Design-Build-Finance-Maintain (DBFM)	Design (D), construction (B), and maintenance (M) are bundled into one procurement and contract with financing (F) provided by the contractor
Design-Build-Finance-Operate (DBFO)	Design (D), construction (B), and operations (O) are bundled into one procurement and contract with financing provided by the contract
Design-Build-Finance-Operate-Maintain (DBFOM)	Design (D), construction (B), maintenance (M), and operations (O) are bundled into one procurement and contract with financing (F) provided by the contractor. This P3 type is also called a concession

Source Martin (2016, p. 3)

Table 4.15 Types of P3s that U.S. State and Local Governments implemented, 1996–2016

P3 Type	Number (Percent)
Design-Build	119 (53.9%)
Design-Build-Finance	19 (8.6%)
Design-Build-Operate and Design-Build-Maintain	32 (14.5%)
Design-Build-Finance-Operate, Design-Build-Finance-Maintain, and Design-Build-Finance-Operate-Maintain	51 (23.1%)
Total	221 (100%)

Source Martin (2016, p. 4)

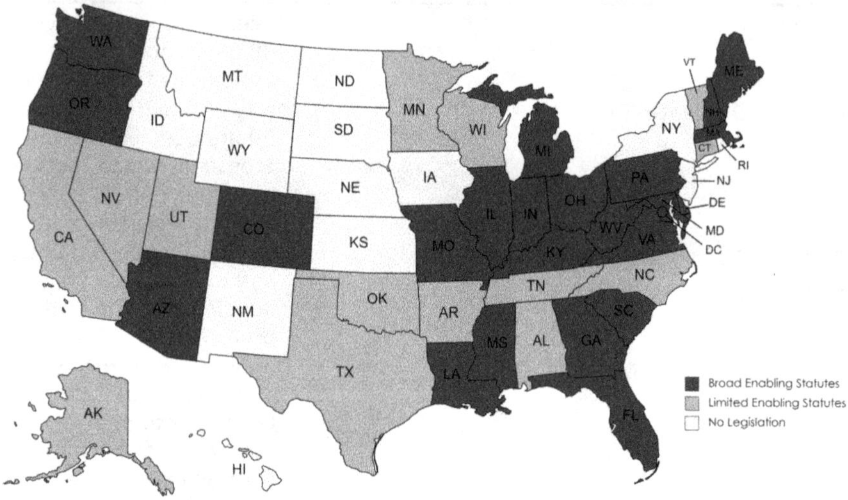

Fig. 4.19 Map of state P3s legislation for transportation projects (*Notes* "Broad" authority means state statutes that authorize a number of agencies and/or a number of eligible projects. "Limited" authority means state statutes that are written for specific projects and/or limited to eligible projects [i.e., for toll roads only or select agencies]. *Data Source* U.S. Department of Transportation [2018]. https://www.fhwa.dot.gov/ipd/p3/legislation/)

transportation P3-enabling statutes range from project-specific authority to a limited authority based on project scope, size, or type to broad comprehensive frameworks for P3 agreements.

Research on U.S. State P3-Enabling Legislation

- Geddes and Wagner (2013) utilize 13 key elements of PPP enabling laws to develop an index reflecting the degree to which a state's law is encouraging or discouraging of private infrastructure investment and then explore why states pass such laws, and why some states pass legislation that is relatively more favorable to private investment. The authors find that Texas, Virginia, Georgia, and Florida have very favorable P3-enabling legislation. Moreover, based on a panel data analysis of 50 American states from 1988 to 2008, the authors conform that infrastructure demand factor (vehicle registration growth and greater traffic congestion) and political factor (political agreement between a state's executive and legislative branches) increase the likelihood of passage of P3-enabling law. Meanwhile, traffic congestion, growth in per capita income, and the percent of Republicans in state Houses increase a P3-enabling law's favorability to private investment.
- Albalate et al. (2020) perform the first comprehensive empirical assessment of the impact of adopting P3-enabling laws on the utilization of private investment for 50 American states from 1988 to 2016. Their empirical analysis reveals that the improved legal frameworks offered by P3-enabling laws are successful in attracting private capital to transportation projects because P3 laws mitigate uncertainty in contracts and lower transaction costs. In addition, they further find that P3 law provisions such as exemptions from property taxes, exemptions from extant procurement laws, and confidentiality protections have a significant effect on attracting private investment.

Source Geddes, R. R., & Wagner, B. L. (2013). Why do US states adopt public–private partnership enabling legislation? *Journal of Urban Economics, 78*, 30–41.

Albalate, D., Bel, G., & Geddes, R. R. (2020). Do public-private-partnership-enabling laws increase private investment in transportation infrastructure? *The Journal of Law and Economics, 63*(1), 43–70.

According to Public Works Financing, P3s were used to help finance and build at least 171 transportation projects for a total of $111 billion between 1996 and 2016 in the U.S. (Fig. 4.20). In general, use of PPPs has increased over time, especially during and after the Great Recession of 2009. As indicated in Table 4.16, Florida and Texas are the top two states that have frequently used P3s to finance state highway projects.

Advantages and Disadvantages: The main advantages of P3s include: (1) shifting project finance risks and long-term operations and maintenance responsibilities to the private sector, (2) leveraging private capital and tapping private sector expertise, and (3) avoiding more debt issuance and preserve bond capacity. However, the significant disadvantages of P3s are: (1) complicated contracts and complex negotiations, (2) requiring a high degree of

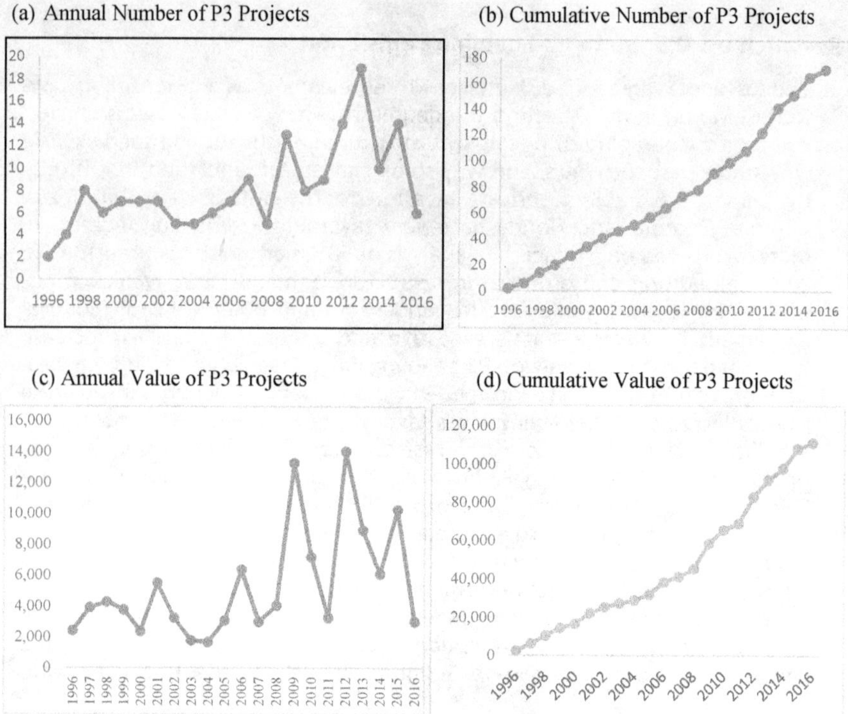

Fig. 4.20 State highway P3s projects in the U.S. (1996–2016) (*Data Source* Public Works Financing Newsletter)

Table 4.16 Top ten states for using highway P3 projects (1996–2016)

State	Rank	Total number of P3 project	Total investment of P3 project (million)	Share in total state P3 projects	Share in total state P3 investment
Florida	1	24	10,419	16.40%	12.00%
Texas	2	22	15,816	14.50%	13.14%
North Carolina	3	13	2,933	8.90%	3.40%
Virginia	4	12	8,421	8.20%	9.70%
Washington	5	7	7,397	4.80%	8.50%
South Carolina	6	6	2,144	4.10%	2.50%
Massachusetts	7	6	1,504	4.10%	1.70%
Utah	8	5	1,806	3.40%	2.10%
Minnesota	9	5	960	3.40%	1.10%
California	10	4	8,838	2.70%	10.20%

Data Source Public Works Financing Newsletter. Major Projects Database

expertise in-house or hiring consultants, (3) demanding huge efforts of enforcement and monitoring contracts, and (4) the typical long-term nature of contracts and loss of public control and flexibility.

Example: The Port Miami Tunnel project is an example of a successful P3 that uses the design-build-finance-operate-and-maintain model. It opened on August 3, 2014. Under a 35-year concession agreement, the Florida DOT, in partnership with Miami-Dade County and the city of Miami, made milestone payments to the concessionaire (MAT Concessionaire LLC) during the construction period. After the project construction, the Florida DOT makes availability payments (capped at $32.5 million per year) to the concessionaire; these payments are contingent on service quality. The tunnel will be returned to the Florida DOT in 2044. The total cost of design and construction is $668.5 million. Florida DOT shared half of the capital design and construction costs and assumed all the operations and maintenance costs. The remaining half of the project capital cost is paid by Miami-Dade County and the city of Miami.

4.5.2 Privatization

Description: Privatization is a controversial topic. Privatization covers a wide set of arrangements where private sector organizations contract with governments for the delivery of services. In the infrastructure area, privatization means the transfer of an infrastructure asset owned and operated by governments to a private party through a sale or long-term lease (Megginson & Netter, 2001). In these arrangements, governments give up direct control and ownership in return for private payment for the operation of infrastructure services. Privatization can save the government money, leverage private sector financial resources and expertise, and improve infrastructure services. But it has many challenges and can be politically controversial.

Since the late 1980s, governments in both developed and developing countries have started to privatize many state-owned enterprises, including infrastructure sectors such as railroads, seaports, airports, toll roads, electricity, and telecommunication infrastructure. Some of these infrastructure facilities were sold to investors, in whole or in part. In the U.S, a significant amount of infrastructure is owned and operated by the private sector containing most energy production infrastructure, electric & gas utility infrastructure, and a portion of water and wastewater infrastructure. These infrastructure assets may be held through publicly traded corporations or master limited partnerships (in the case of energy), or they may be owned directly by private businesses (Poole, 2021).

Advantages and Disadvantages: The main advantages of privatization include: (1) obtaining up-front payment and quick construction of the facility and (2) transferring government risks to private and nonprofit sectors. However, the significant disadvantages of privatization are: (1) complicated contracts and complex negotiations, (2) demanding efforts to enforce and monitor contracts, and (3) loss of public control and flexibility.

Examples: The city of Chicago, Illinois, pioneered the privatization of municipal infrastructure. In 2005, the city of Chicago leased the Chicago Skyway, a 7.8-mile city-owned toll road, for 99 years to private investors for $1.83 billion. The concessionaire was responsible for operating and maintenance costs and collecting toll revenues.

In 2006, the city of Chicago and the Chicago Park District leased four city-owned downtown parking garages for 99 years to Morgan Stanley for $563 million. The main reason for leasing parking garages was that parking fee revenues were insufficient to pay for the city's parking debt service. In 2009, the city of Chicago also leased its 36,000 on-street meters for 75 years to private investors for $1.2 billion.

Although these three high-profile privatizations generated billions of dollars in one-time asset lease proceeds, they were controversial. Leasing the parking facilities resulted in an immediate increase in parking costs for residents and businesses. In most Chicago neighborhoods, parking meter rates increased from 25 cents an hour to $2 an hour. Downtown parking meter rates increased from $3 to $6.50 an hour. In addition, Chicago's parking meter privatization was criticized by some as an unfavorable deal because the city could have earned $1.5 billion instead of $1.2 billion if it had kept its parking meters and raised meter rates to the same levels as the concessionaire. See Sects. 5.5.2 and 5.5.3 for a more detailed discussion.

4.5.3 Infrastructure Investment Funds (IIFs)

Description: An infrastructure investment fund generally refers to an entity in which large investors—such as pension funds, sovereign wealth funds, private insurance companies, and investment banks—pool their financial resources and employ experienced fund managers to invest their fund equity into various kinds of infrastructure assets (Poole, 2015, p. 1). Infrastructure investment funds generally seek to make investment in either in infrastructure that has been privatized (or has always been in the private sector) or in the special purpose governmental entities established to operate and manage infrastructure under long-term public–private partnerships. Infrastructure investment funds have shown strong interest in long-term infrastructure projects with low-risk investment, a reasonable return, and stable cash flow.

It is estimated that infrastructure investment funds have raised about $300 billion of equity capital from 2004 to 2014 (Poole, 2015). Institutional investors comprise the major source of equity capital for infrastructure funds. A study by Standard & Poor's Ratings Service (2015) highlights the potential of institutional investors to help close the global infrastructure financing gap, estimating that there is a potential to close this gap by as much as 20% from 2015 to 2030. Every year, *Infrastructure Investor* publishes a table of the amounts raised by the 50 largest infrastructure investment funds over the latest five-year period. Table 4.17 shows those funds and the five-year total each had raised by November 2021.

Advantages and Disadvantages: The main advantages of infrastructure investment funds include: (1) quickly obtaining up-front capital, (2) attracting new and global private investors, and (3) a long-term and stable private equity source. However, the significant disadvantages of infrastructure investment funds are: (1) increased project financing costs due to higher return interest rate with private equity and (2) potentially higher turnover of institutional fund managers.

Example: In 2015, the Dallas, Texas, Police, and Fire Pension System (DPFP) had an infrastructure asset allocation of $197 million, equal to 6.7% of its nearly $3 billion total assets. The DPFP reported that a part of these infrastructure assets was invested in hospital and water treatment plant projects in Asia and in managed highway lanes in Texas.

4.5.4 Private and Nonprofit Philanthropic Partners

Description: Philanthropic organizations, private foundations, and a range of nonprofit organizations show a growing interest in investing in local infrastructure. These organizations can make either donations or grants with a charitable purpose to support building or operating local infrastructure (see Table 4.18). For instance, over the past decade, the Rockefeller Foundation has invested more than a half-billion dollars to improve the infrastructure resilience of communities. In addition, foundations can sometimes

Table 4.17 Top 50 Infrastructure Investment Funds Worldwide (as of November 2021)

Rank	Infrastructure investment fund manager	Headquarters	5-year total ($B)
1	Macquarie Asset Management	UK	76
2	Global Infrastructure Partners	USA	65
3	Brookfield Asset Management	Canada	52
4	KKR	USA	47
5	EQT Partners	Sweden	37
6	Stonepeak Infrastructure Partners	USA	31
7	I Squared Capital	USA	22
8	BlackRock	USA	22
9	IFM Investors	Australia	21
10	AMP Capital	Australia	20
11	Antin Infrastructure Partners	France	18
12	Blackstone	USA	17
13	First Sentier Investors	Australia	17
14	Copenhagen Infrastructure Partners	Denmark	15
15	DigitalBridge Group	USA	15
16	Morgan Stanley Infrastructure Partners	USA	12
17	Ardian	France	12
18	Actis	UK	10
19	Partners Group	Switzerland	9
20	Energy Capital Partners	USA	9
21	DIF Capital Partners	Netherlands	9
22	Meridiam	France	8
23	InfraVia Capital Partners	France	8
24	Greencoat Capital	UK	7
25	Dalmore Capital Limited	UK	7
26	QIC Limited	Australia	7
27	DWS	Germany	6
28	Equitix	UK	6
29	Vauban Infrastructure Partners	France	6
30	AIP Management	Denmark	6
31	The Carlyle Group	USA	6
32	Axium Infrastructure	Canada	6
33	F2i Sgr SpA	Italy	6
34	InfraRed Capital Partners	UK	6
35	InfraCapital	YJ	5

(continued)

Table 4.17 (continued)

Rank	Infrastructure investment fund manager	Headquarters	5-year total ($B)
36	The National Investment and Infrastructure Fund	India	5
37	IPI Partners	USA	5
38	Grain Management	USA	4
39	China Merchants Capital	China	4
40	Swiss Life Asset Managers	Germany	4
41	Basalt Infrastructure Partners	UK	4
42	Arcus Infrastructure Partners	UK	4
43	Capital Dynamics	Switzerland	4
44	Energy Infrastructure Partners	Germany	4
45	Argo Infrastructure Partners	USA	4
46	Goldman Sachs	USA	4
47	GCM Grosvenor	USA	4
48	Mirova	France	4
49	Amber Infrastructure Group	UK	4
50	iCON Infrastructure	UK	3

Data Source Infrastructure Investor. November 1, 2021. https://www.infrastructureinvestor.com/download-the-november-2021-issue-of-infrastructure-investor/

Table 4.18 Examples of grants to the water infrastructure sector from philanthropic organizations (2001–2014)

Philanthropic organizations	Total amount granted ($)
The Bill & Melinda Gates Foundation	655.3 million
Conrad N. Hilton Foundation	126.7 million
The Coca-Cola Foundation, Inc	104.1 million
Howard G. Buffett Foundation	76.2 million
Queen Elizabeth Diamond Trust	62.3 million
The PepsiCo Foundation, Inc	46.8 million
Caterpillar Foundation	23 million

Source Ajami et al. (2018, p. 19)

make program-related investments to support their philanthropic mission and leverage their donations, such as supporting local affordable housing and community development projects, rehabilitating historic buildings, and preserving open space (U.S. Bipartisan Policy Center, 2016). In these cases, philanthropic investments allow the recipient to borrow capital at lower rates or simply borrow less. The repayment or return of equity can be recycled for future charitable infrastructure investment.

Advantages and Disadvantages: The main advantages of private and nonprofit philanthropic partners include: (1) attracting new investors from nonprofit and private sectors, (2) attracting new investors from nonprofit and private sectors, (3) leveraging a large amount of financing quickly, and (4) preserving public funding capacity. However, the significant disadvantages of private and nonprofit philanthropic partners are (1) the application process and the requirement to compete for limited funding sources and (2) the imposition of donor requirements and control.

Examples: In Dallas, Texas, private corporate and individual donors contributed to the design and construction of the Margaret Hunt Hill Bridge in 2013. Private donations contributed \$16 million of the \$182 million project cost, including \$12 million from Hunt Petroleum.

In Detroit, Michigan, a coalition of private sector philanthropic and business leaders committed \$100 million in 2014 toward building and operating a new streetcar line along Woodward Avenue in the downtown area. The total estimated project cost was \$137 million, with additional funding from state and local governments.

4.5.5 Crowdfunding

Description: Crowdfunding is the sourcing of small amounts of funds from a large group of individuals (Ross, 2015). It is an emerging method and has become increasingly popular for raising donations for relatively small civic infrastructure projects. Crowdfunding builds a connection between entrepreneurs whose goal is to raise the fund (the fundraisers) and investors (the crowd) who are willing to invest small amounts through an Internet-based intermediary (an online platform). In general, there are three main types of crowdfunding (Shneor, 2020):

- Donation-based crowdfunding. It is the most well-known type of crowdfunding. It means creating a fundraising online platform and ask individuals to donate a small amount of money. As a result, a lot of small donations will provide the funding for infrastructure projects.
- Equity crowdfunding. It allows people to invest in private early-stage startups via online platforms and gives invested people partial ownership of the infrastructure projects.
- Debt (rewards)-based crowdfunding. It involves asking a crowd to donate to a project or business in exchange for a future financial return.

Crowdfunding has been successful in funding small municipal infrastructure projects. In the U.S., a total of more than $10.5 million has been raised by more than 1,200 civic crowdfunding campaigns since 2010. More than 60% of these civic crowdfunding campaigns have successfully reached or exceeded their target amount (Gasparro, 2015). The successful projects include the Arapahoe Protected Bike Lanes in Denver, the Hampline in Memphis, the Liverpool Flyover, and the Denver mini bond. The crowdfunding process is tailored to each project. Table 4.19 provides comparison of common civic crowdfunding platforms.

Advantages and Disadvantages: The main advantages of crowdfunding include: (1) reducing the capital costs associated with privately financed infrastructure, (2) funding small infrastructure projects quickly, (3) increasing political will to support infrastructure development, and (4) involving local citizens in a civic investment. However, the significant disadvantages of crowdfunding are: (1) it may be difficult to fund large infrastructure projects, (2) funding campaigns may require significant resources (money and time), and (3) the risk of online platform closure and failure.

Examples: In 2013, the city of Memphis, Tennessee, issued a crowdfunding campaign to help build a local bike transportation project. This is the first American bike transportation project that will be paid for in part by crowdfunding. A total of $75,000 was raised to cover part of the project cost.

In 2014, Denver, Colorado, used crowdfunding to raise $36,085 from 250 individuals and small businesses to fund the remaining amount needed to build the Arapahoe protected bike lane project. This crowdfunding effort not only reached the financing goals but also raised citizens' awareness about bicycling (Both projects are discussed in depth in Sect. 5.6.4).

Table 4.19 Comparison of civic crowdfunding platforms

Platform	Platform Type	Primary Service Area	Project Risk Level	Who Fundraises?	Contributors Receive	Who Receives & Spends the Funds?
Neighborly	For-Profit	U.S.	Low	Government	Financial return via municipal bonds	Government
Citizinvestor (Defunct as of October 2017)	For-Profit	U.S	Low	Government (or Official Partner)	Tax deduction	Government
Spacehive	Nonprofit	United Kingdom	High	Community Members	N/A	Project Creators
Patronicity	Nonprofit	U.S	High	Community Members	Tax deduction	Project Creators
Ioby	Nonprofit	U.S.	High	Community Members	Tax deduction	Project Creators

Source Weinberger (2020, p. 60)

References

Agrawal, A. W., Nixon, H., & Hooper, A. M. (2016). *Public perception of mileage-based user fees*. https://www.nap.edu/catalog/23401/public-perception-of-mileage-based-user-fees. Accessed 3 September 2021.

Ajami, N., Habicht, H., Fewell, B., Lattimer, T., & Ng, T. (2018). *Water finance: The imperative for water security and economic growth*. https://waterinthewest.stanford.edu/sites/default/files/Water_Finance_Water_Security_Economic_G rowth.pdf. Accessed 24 November 2021.

Albalate, D., Bel, G., & Geddes, R. R. (2020). Do public-private-partnership-enabling laws increase private investment in transportation infrastructure? *The Journal of Law and Economics, 63*(1), 43–70.

American Society of Civil Engineers (ASCE). (2021). *The America's 2021 infrastructure report card*. https://infrastructurereportcard.org/making-the-grade/. Accessed 3 September 2021.

ASCE. (2019). *Policy statement 496: Innovative finance for transportation project*. https://www.asce.org/issues-and-advocacy/public-policy/policy-statement-496---innovative-financing-for-transportation-projects/ Accessed 3 September 2021.

BATIC Institute: An AASHTO Center for Excellence. (2021). *State Infrastructure Bank (SIB) Legislation*. http://www.financingtransportation.org/funding_f inancing/legislation_regulations/state_legislation/sibs.aspx. Accessed 7 December 2021.

Berlin, G. L. (2016). *Learning from experience: A guide to social impact bond investing*. https://www.mdrc.org/sites/default/files/Learning_from_Experie nce_SIB.pdf. Accessed 24 November 2021.

Bloomberg. (2021). *Biden Spending Plan Seen Jolting Muni Green-Bond Sales to Record*. https://www.bloomberg.com/news/articles/2021-04-20/biden-spending-plan-seen-jolting-muni-green-bond-sales-to-record. Accessed 16 November 2021.

Brand, M. W., Quesnel, K., Saksa, P., Ulibarri, N., et al. (2021). Environmental impact bonds: A common framework and looking ahead. *Journal of Environmental Research: Infrastructure and Sustainability, 1*(2), 1–18.

Brill, A. (2017). *Carbon tax policy: A conservative dialogue on pro-growth opportunities*. Alliance for Market Solutions. https://amsresearch.org/report/carbon-tax-pol icy-a-conservative-dialogue-on-pro-growth-opportunities/. Accessed 3 September 2021

Brookings Institution. (2021). *Global Impact Bonds Database*. https://www.bro okings.edu/research/social-and-development-impact-bonds-by-the-numbers/. Accessed 13 November 2021.

Chen, C. (2016a). Innovative infrastructure financing tools. In D. L. Smith & J. B. Justice (Eds.), *Encyclopedia of public administration and policy*. Taylor & Francis Group Press.

Chen, C. (2016b). Banking on infrastructure: Exploring the fiscal impact of state infrastructure bank loans on leveraging state and local transportation investment. *Public Budgeting and Finance, 36*(3), 94–113.

Chen, C., & Afonso, W. B. (2021). The adoption of local option fuel taxes: Evidence from Florida counties. *Public Budgeting & Finance, 41*(1), 51–75.

Connecticut Governor's Council on Climate Change. (2020). *A Report of the financing and funding adaptation and resilience working group*. https://portal.ct.gov/-/media/DEEP/climatechange/GC3/GC3-working-group-reports/GC3_Financing_adaptation_resilience_draft_report_public_comment_092120.pdf. Accessed 3 September 2021.

Edison Electric Institute. (2018). *Electric vehicle sales forecast and the charging infrastructure required through 2030*. https://www.edisonfoundation.net/-/media/Files/IEI/publications/IEI_EEI-EV-Forecast-Report_Nov2018.ashx. Accessed 3 September 2021.

Gasparro, K. (2015). *Funding municipal infrastructure: Integrating project finance and crowdfunding*. https://gpc.stanford.edu/sites/default/files/wp87.pdf. Accessed 3 September 2021.

Geddes, R. R., & Wagner, B. L. (2013). Why do US states adopt public–private partnership enabling legislation? *Journal of Urban Economics, 78*, 30–41.

Goldman, T., Corbett, S., & Wachs, M. (2001). *Local option transportation taxes in the United States: Part One: Issues and trends*. https://escholarship.org/content/qt546317dh/qt546317dh_noSplash_31ac3ec07071d13ddc0b05eb6b3f09c9.pdf. Accessed 12 September 2021.

Goldman, T., & Wachs, M. (2003). A quiet revolution in transportation finance: The rise of local option transportation taxes. *Transportation Quarterly, 57*(1), 19–32.

Greer, R. A. (2020). A review of public water infrastructure financing in the United States. *Wires Water, 7*(5), 1–13. https://doi.org/10.1002/wat2.1472

Gustasson-Wright, E. (2020). *What is the size and scope of the impact bonds market?* https://www.brookings.edu/wp-content/uploads/2020/09/Impact_Bonds-Brief_1-FINAL.pdf. Accessed 3 September 2021.

Harvard Kennedy School. (2013).*Social impact bonds: A guide for state and local governments*. http://govlab.hks.harvard.edu/files/siblab/files/social-impact-bonds-a-guide-for-state-and%20local-governments.pdf. Accessed 3 September 2021.

Hemenway, C. (2013). *GC securities, rms involved in first ever cat bond for storm surge*. https://www.propertycasualty360.com/2013/08/01/gc-securities-rms-involved-in-first-ever-cat-bond/. Accessed 3 September 2021.

Infrastructure Investor. (2021, November 1). https://www.infrastructureinvestor.com/download-the-november-2021-issue-of-infrastructure-investor/. Accessed 22 November 2021

International Capital Market Association. (2021). *The green bond principles (GBP) 2021*. https://www.icmagroup.org/sustainable-finance/the-principles-guidelines-and-handbooks/green-bond-principles-gbp/. Accessed 3 September 2021.

Litman, T. (2021). *Local funding options for public transportation.* https://vtpi.org/tranfund.pdf. Accessed 3 September 2021.

Martin, L. (2016). *Public-private partnerships (P3s): What local government managers need to know.* https://icma.org/sites/default/files/18-109%20Public-Private%20Partnerships-P3s%20White%20Paper_web%20FINAL.pdf. Accessed 3 September 2021.

Megginson, W. L., & Netter, J. M. (2001). From state to market: A survey of empirical studies on privatization. *Journal of Economic Literature, 39*(2), 321–389.

Mullin, M., & Daley, D. M. (2018). Multilevel instruments for infrastructure investment: Evaluating state revolving funds for water. *Policy Studies Journal, 46*(3), 629–650.

Murray, B., & Rivers, N. (2015). British Columbia's revenue-neutral carbon tax: A review of the latest "grand experiment" in environmental policy. *Energy Policy, 86*, 674–683.

National Conference of State Legislatures. (2017). *P3 infrastructure delivery: principles for state legislature.* https://www.ncsl.org/Portals/1/documents/transportation/P3_Infrastructure_080117.pdf. Accessed 3 September 2021.

National Conference of State Legislatures. (2021a). *State road user charge toolkit.* https://www.ncsl.org/research/transportation/state-road-user-charge-pilot-results-and-legislative-action.aspx. Accessed 3 September 2021.

National Conference of State Legislatures. (2021b). *Special fees on plug-in hybrid and electric vehicles.* https://www.ncsl.org/research/energy/new-fees-on-hybrid-and-electric-vehicles.aspx. Accessed 3 September 2021.

National League of Cities. (2016). *Paying for local infrastructure in a new era of federalism.* https://www.nlc.org/wp-content/uploads/2016/12/NLC_2016_Infrastructure_Report.pdf. Accessed 3 September 2021.

Ohio Department of Transportation (2021). *2020 state infrastructure bank (SIB) annual report.* https://www.transportation.ohio.gov/wps/portal/gov/odot/programs/state-infrastructure-bank/sib-reports/sib-report-2020. Accessed 20 January 2022.

Oregon Department of Transportation. (2007). *Oregon's mileage fee concept and road user fee pilot program.* https://www.myorego.org/wp-content/uploads/2017/07/RUFPP_finalreport.pdf. Accessed 3 September 2021.

Oregon Department of Transportation (2017). *The Oregon's road usage charge.* https://www.oregon.gov/ODOT/Programs/RUF/IP-Road%20Usage%20Evaluation%20Book%20WEB_4-26.pdf. Accessed 3 September 2021.

Poole, R. (2015). *Annual privatization report 2015: Air transportation.* http://reason.org/files/apr-2015-airtransportation.pdf. Accessed 3 September 2021.

Poole, R. W. (2021). *Annual privatization report: Transportation finance.* https://reason.org/wpcontent/uploads/annual-privatization-report-2021-transportation-finance.pdf. Accessed 20 January 2022.

Puentes, R., & Thompson, J. (2012). *Banking on infrastructure: Enhancing state revolving funds for transportation.* Brookings-Rockefeller: Project on State and

Metropolitan Innovation. https://www.brookings.edu/research/papers/2012/09/12-state-infrastructure-investment-puentes. Accessed 20 January 2022.

Quantified Ventures. (2018). *Sharing risk, rewarding outcomes: The environmental impact bond*. https://www.quantifiedventures.com/blog/what-is-an-environmental-impact-bond. Accessed 3 September 2021.

Ross, B. (2015). *Public policy benefits of a crowdfunding enhanced P3 model*. https://www.infrashares.com/blog-detail/21. Accessed 3 September 2021.

Rudd, T., Nicoletti, E., Misner, K., & Bonsu, J. (2013). *Financing promising evidence-based programs: Early lessons from the New York City Social Impact Bond*. MDRC. https://www.mdrc.org/publication/financing-promising-evidence-based-programs. Accessed 22 November 2021.

Shneor, R. (2020). Crowdfunding models, strategies, and choices between them. In R. Shneor, L. Zhao, & B. T. Flåten (Eds.), *Advances in Crowdfunding* (pp. 21–42). Palgrave Macmillan.

Standard & Poor's Ratings Service. (2015). *Global Infrastructure: How to fill a $500 billion hole*. http://www.standardandpoors.com/spf/upload/Ratings_EMEA/HowToFIllAn500BillionHoleJan162014.pd. Accessed 3 September 2021.

The City of Atlanta. (2016). *TSPLOST and MARTA referenda*. https://www.atlantaga.gov/government/mayor-s-office/projects-and-initiatives/tsplost-and-marta-referenda. Accessed 3 September 2021.

The City of New York. (2012). *Bringing social impact bonds to New York city*. http://www.nyc.gov/html/om/pdf/2012/sib_media_presentation_080212.pdf. Accessed 3 September 2021.

The National Surface Transportation Infrastructure Commission. (2009). *Paying our way: A new framework for transportation finance*. https://financecommission.dot.gov/. Accessed 3 September 2021.

The Washington D.C. Water. (No date). *Fact sheet: DC water environmental impact bond results- successful*. https://dcwater.com/sites/default/files/finance/eib-factsheet.pdf. Accessed 27 September 2021.

U.S. Bipartisan Policy Center. (2016). *Bridging the gap together: A new model to modernize U.S. infrastructure*. http://cdn.bipartisanpolicy.org/wpcontent/uploads/2016/05/BPC-NewInfrastructure-Model.pdf. Accessed 3 September 2021.

U.S. Congressional Research Service. (2018). *The railroad rehabilitation and improvement financing (RRIF) program*. https://sgp.fas.org/crs/misc/R44028.pdf. Accessed 3 September 2021.

U.S. Congressional Research Service. (2020). *Funding and financing highways and public transportation*. https://sgp.fas.org/crs/misc/R45350.pdf. Accessed 3 September 2021.

U.S. DOT. (2012). *Risk assessment for public-private partnerships: A primer*. https://www.fhwa.dot.gov/ipd/pdfs/p3/p3_risk_assessment_primer_122612.PDF. Accessed 3 September 2021.

U.S. DOT. (2016a). *TIFIA portfolio update*. https://cms.dot.gov/sites/dot.gov/files/docs/TIFIA_Portfolio_Update_March2016_0.pdf. Accessed 3 September 2021.

U.S. DOT. (2016b). *State infrastructure banks*. https://www.fhwa.dot.gov/ipd/pdfs/fact_sheets/techtools_SIBs.pdf. Accessed 27 September 2021.

U.S. DOT. (2016c). *Grant anticipation revenue vehicles (GARVEEs)*. https://www.fhwa.dot.gov/ipd/pdfs/fact_sheets/techtools_GARVEES.pdf. Accessed 3 September 2021.

U.S. DOT. (2017). *State Infrastructure Bank Best Practices*. https://www.fhwa.dot.gov/ipd/pdfs/finance/sib_best_practices_1117.pdf. Accessed 27 September 2021.

U.S. DOT. (2018). *State P3 legislation*. https://www.fhwa.dot.gov/ipd/p3/legislation/. Accessed 27 September 2021.

U.S. DOT. (2019). *Value capture: Capitalizing on the value created by transportation*. https://www.fhwa.dot.gov/ipd/pdfs/value_capture/value_capture_implementation_manual_2019.pdf. Accessed 2 September 2021.

U.S. DOT. (2021a). *TIFIA credit program overview*. https://www.transportation.gov/buildamerica/financing/tifia/tifia-credit-program-overview. Accessed 3 September 2021.

U.S. DOT. (2021b). *Current GARVEE activity*. https://www.fhwa.dot.gov/ipd/finance/tools_programs/federal_debt_financing/garvees/garvee_state_by_state.aspx. Accessed 21 November 2021.

U.S. FHWA Center for Innovative Finance Support. (2021). *State Infrastructure Banks (SIBs)*. https://www.fhwa.dot.gov/ipd/finance/tools_programs/federal_credit_assistance/sibs/. Accessed 7 December 2021.

U.S. Environmental Protection Agency. (2010a). *Clean water state revolving fund programs 2009 annual report*. https://nepis.epa.gov/Exe/ZyPURL.cgi?Dockey=P100DP65.TXT. Accessed 3 September 2021.

U.S. Environmental Protection Agency. (2010b). *Drinking water state revolving fund: 2009 annual report*. https://nepis.epa.gov/Exe/ZyPURL.cgi?Dockey=P100DP65.TXT. Accessed 3 September 2021.

U.S. Environmental Protection Agency. (2013). *Drinking water infrastructure needs survey and assessment*. https://www.epa.gov/sites/production/files/2015-07/documents/epa816r13006.pdf. Accessed 3 September 2021.

U.S. EPA. (2016). *What is WIFIA?* https://www.epa.gov/sites/default/files/2021-03/documents/wifia_program_overview_factsheet.pdf. Accessed 3 September 2021.

U.S. EPA. (2018). *WIFIA Project Loan—Omaha, Nebraska*. https://www.epa.gov/sites/default/files/2018-06/documents/omaha_wifiaprojectfactsheet_loanclose.pdf. Accessed 3 September 2021.

U.S. EPA. (2020). *Sources of greenhouse gas emissions*. https://www.epa.gov/ghgemissions/sources-greenhouse-gas-emissions. Accessed 3 September 2021.

U.S. EPA. (2021a). *WIFIA Closed Loans*. https://www.epa.gov/wifia/wifia-closed-loans. Accessed 21 November 2021.

U.S. EPA. (2021b). *CWSRF National Information Management System Reports*. https://www.epa.gov/cwsrf/clean-water-state-revolving-fund-cwsrf-national-information-management-system-reports. Accessed 13 November 2021.

U.S. EPA. (2021c). *DWSRF National Information Management System Reports*. https://www.epa.gov/dwsrf/drinking-water-state-revolving-fund-national-information-management-system-reports. Accessed 13 November 2021.

U.S. Department of Treasury. (2014). *Expanding our nation's infrastructure through innovative financing*. https://www.ncsl.org/Portals/1/documents/transportation/P3_Infrastructure_080117.pdf. Accessed 3 September 2021.

Vaijhala, S., & Rhodes, J. (2018). Resilience Bonds: A business-model for resilient infrastructure. *Field Actions Science Reports, 18*, 58–63.

Walczak, J. (2019). *Local income taxes in 2019*. https://files.taxfoundation.org/20190730170302/Local-Income-Taxes-in-20191.pdf. Accessed 3 September 2021.

Weinberger, D. J. (2020). Civic crowdfunding, equity, and the role of government. In O. Gajda, D. Marom, & T. Wright (Eds.), *The Book of Crowdasset: Crowdfunding for policymakers* (pp. 47–87). World Scientific Publishing Company.

White House. (2014). *Fact sheet: Build America infrastructure investment summit*. https://obamawhitehouse.archives.gov/the-press-office/2014/09/09/fact-sheet-build-america-infrastructure-investment-summit. Accessed 3 September 2021.

Wisconsin Policy Forum. (2018). *Local governments turn to "wheel taxes" as other revenues lag*. https://wispolicyforum.org/wp-content/uploads/2018/06/Focus_18_10.pdf. Accessed 3 September 2021.

Yusuf, J. E., O'Connell, L., Hackbart, M., & Liu, G. (2010). State infrastructure banks and borrowing costs for transportation projects. *Public Finance Review, 38*(6), 682–709.

5

Case Studies in Innovative Infrastructure Financing

This chapter presents in-depth case analyses of six various types of innovative infrastructure financing with the goal of offering best practices and lessons for state and local government professionals in considering the use of innovative infrastructure financing. The first section discusses value capture. The second section presents state infrastructure banks. The third section describes Green, Social and Sustainable Bonds. The fourth section discusses Public-Private Partnerships. The fifth section presents privatization. The last section describes crowdfunding . Each section includes a concise description of each method, the use of this method, two or more cases illustrating the method, as well as lessons learned.

5.1 Value Capture

5.1.1 Description

Value capture refers to any strategy where a public agency "captures" a portion of an increase in property values resulting from an infrastructure improvement to help pay for the infrastructure itself (U.S. DOT, 2019). Value capture often takes different forms. Across the U.S., the most common forms of value capture are developer contributions, special assessment and tax districts, tax increment financing (TIF), joint development, and naming rights. Value capture is widely considered as one potential new revenue source

C. Chen and J. R. Bartle, *Innovative Infrastructure Finance*, https://doi.org/10.1007/978-3-030-91411-0_5

that can be tapped to offer funding for a variety of state and local infrastructure projects (Zhao et al., 2012). This section focuses on one of the most important mechanisms of value capture—joint development. According to Zhao et al. (2012), joint development is "a formal arrangement between the public sector and private entities such that the private entities share some costs of infrastructure improvement or contribute some benefits back to the public sector based on a mutual recognition of the benefits of such infrastructure improvement" (p. 5). There are three basic characteristics in joint development (Renaissance Planning Group, 2014, pp. 7–8):

- A joint development project is mutually beneficial to its public and private sector participants.
- Joint development is opportunistic and takes advantage of specific opportunities at a location and the specific objectives and capabilities of the public agency and private developers involved.
- Joint development involves a financial transaction in which the project will include revenue or cost sharing between the public agency and a private partner.

In practice, the most common joint development arrangements range from ground leases to air-rights development, transit station interface, or connection improvement. Public transit agencies have heavily used joint development to capture some of the economic value created by the transit systems and use the funds to help finance transit operations (so-called Transit-Oriented Development [TOD]). In addition to transit, joint development agreements have also been used to implement highway improvements and parking projects. Three primary benefits of joint development include that it produces a new revenue source for the public agency, that it shares the cost of public infrastructure construction and operation between public and private sectors, and that it may stimulate transit ridership (Renaissance Planning Group, 2014).

5.1.2 Joint Development in Miami

Project: Miami-Dade County, Florida, is one of the few governments in the U.S. with extensive experience in implementing joint TOD projects. This county planned and constructed the Metrorail system with a large amount of land surrounding the transit stations under the control of Miami-Dade Transit (MDT).

In 1994, a joint development project in the Dadeland North Metrorail Station was initiated. Private developers were attracted by the proximity of Dadeland North Station to the nearby Dadeland Mall and the general absence of available land in the area and approached MDT about developing the Dadeland North Station area. The private developers and MDT agreed to a 99-year land lease in 1994. Under the joint development agreement, MDT receives a guaranteed minimum land rent and a gross rent payment based on the percentage of development revenues: 5% of the first $7 million, and 5.5% of above $7 million. MDT can penalize the developers for construction delays (delayed payment $20,000 per month indexed to inflation.) The joint development agreement specified design specifications for transit access. The following Table 5.1 shows the phases and components of this joint development project.

Lessons Learned: The joint development project in North Dadeland Station generated a significant amount of stable revenue—$428,021 in 2010. In addition, this project significantly increased transit ridership. The average weekday ridership at the Dadeland North station has approached 5,000 (Silva et al., 2012). Sharing infrastructure improvement costs is another key benefit that MDT received from joint development. Other lessons learned from this joint development project (Renaissance Planning Group, 2014, pp. 32–33):

- The county's direct control of land surrounding the transit stations reduced political disagreements and layers of administrative approval in the permitting process.

Table 5.1 Dadeland North Station joint development project phases

Phase	Year Opened	Development components
Phase 1	1996	Big Box Retail: 355,000 sq. ft TOD Retail: 9,600 sq. ft Other Retail: 15,600 sq. ft Parking Garage: 1,487 spaces
Phase 2	2000	Apartments: 48 units
Phase 3	2005	Apartments: 110 units Town homes: 10 units Retail: 6,400 sq. ft Parking Garage: 214 spaces
Phase 4	Proposed	Office: 127,000 sq. ft Retail: 8,400 sq. ft Parking Garage: 362 spaces

Source Renaissance Planning Group (2014, p. 30)

- Conduct a market analysis to identify a list of projects where joint development is suitable.
- Develop standard protocols and teams to guide the joint development project from concept to construction.
- Be realistic about the market risk of land development.

In sum, the Dadeland North Station project demonstrates that joint development can be a win-win-win. The private developers have an opportunity to build profitable projects next to transit while the local transit agency obtains stable revenues and additional transit ridership as well as support for economic development. Miami-Dade County transit agency's experience highlights the importance of sound predevelopment planning and marketing and being very clear about goals for the development site.

5.2 State Infrastructure Banks

5.2.1 Description

State infrastructure banks (SIBs) use seed capitalization funds from federal transportation aid and state-matching funds to get started and offer low-interest loans and non-grant forms of credit enhancements to public and private sponsors of state and local transportation projects (Chen, 2016). The state of Ohio was one of eight states selected for designation under the SIB pilot program authorized by the 1995 National Highway System Bill. The Ohio SIB was initially capitalized with $87 million in Federal Title XXIII Highway Funds, a match fund of a $40 million authorization of state general revenue funds from the Ohio State Legislature, and $10 million in state motor fuel tax funds (Ohio DOT, 2021). The objective of the Ohio SIB is to maximize the use of federal and state funds to make direct loans to eligible projects. Repayments are made to the Ohio Department of Transportation (Ohio Department of Transportation, 2011) and then re-loaned to subsequent projects, hence creating a SIB revolving loan program. In Ohio, eligible SIB loan applicants include any public entity, such as counties, cities, villages, townships, boards or commissions, regional transit, and port authorities. The Ohio SIB is one of the most active SIBs in the nation. As of September 30, 2020, the Ohio SIB has issued 252 loans totalling $674.3 million to help local governments build various kinds of transportation projects since the inception of the program in 1997 (ODOT, 2021).

5.2.2 Using SIB for Economic Development

Project: In 2009, the City of Gahanna, Ohio, planned to build an overpass over the Columbus Outerbelt (I-270) to connect an isolated section of Gahanna with the rest of the community. This project was expected to be a boon for local economic development efforts, as the now-connected portion of the town was the last large, undeveloped land available for development. The total project cost was initially estimated to be $8,147,500. The city's involvement with the Ohio SIB program was facilitated through the regional metropolitan planning organization, the Mid-Ohio Regional Planning Commission (MORPC), which allocated attributable federal funds. Each year MORPC receives approximately $33 million of federal funds to use for transportation projects in central Ohio. These funds come from the federal transportation programs: Surface Transportation Program, Congestion Mitigation and Air Quality Improvement Program, and Transportation Alternatives Program.

In 2010, the Ohio SIB awarded a five-year short-term loan of $6,347,508 to the city of Gahanna. The loan interest rate was 3%. The loan was used for the construction of a new 3,000-foot roadway on State Route 317 (Ohio Department of Transportation, 2011). The project included the construction of a new structure over I-270, which tied a new roadway into a Tech Center on the north side of I-270. MORPC handled the bulk of the administrative work related to the SIB loan and paid its share with federal funding. In 2015, the SIB loan was paid off by MORPC and the city of Gahanna.

Lessons Learned: The SIB loan made it possible for the city of Gahanna to complete the work years ahead of the next round of attributable federal funds. In addition, it allowed the city to access capital funds below market interest rates and save on its borrowing costs. To secure SIB loans, state and local government borrowers must submit loan applications and negotiate the structure of the loan term. Sometimes, local borrowers need to collaborate with regional or metropolitan planning organizations on the loan application. It is also important to government applicants to show the public benefits of sponsored projects and their ability to repay the loan. Finally, if a project is funded with federal funds in the SIB program, all Federal regulations (e.g., environmental requirements) must be followed.

5.3 Green, Social and Sustainable Bonds

5.3.1 Description

Green bonds are bonds that finance specific "green" projects that have significant environmental benefits. Entities issuing the bonds (issuers) agree to provide additional disclosures to potential investors to demonstrate alignment with four components of Green Bond Principles (GBP) as articulated by the International Capital Market Association:

- Use of proceeds: The proceeds of the bonds are utilized for eligible green projects (such as described below) and are described in the legal documentation. The projects should be assessed and, where feasible, quantified by the issuer.
- Process for project evaluation and selection: The issuer should communicate to investors the environmental sustainability objectives of the projects, the process of selection, and information on procedures by which the issuer identifies and manages perceived social and environmental risks of the projects.
- Management of proceeds: The proceeds should be tracked by the issuer and, if possible, the use of the proceeds be verified by an external auditor.
- Reporting: Issuers should provide regularly updated information on the use of proceeds. Most issue an annual report. The annual report should include a list of the projects funded by green bonds, a description of the projects, the amounts allocated, and their impact. (International Capital Market Association, 2021a).

The GBP provide broad categories for suitable green activities:

- Renewable energy,
- Energy efficiency,
- Pollution prevention and control,
- Environmentally sustainable management of living natural resources and land use,
- Terrestrial and aquatic biodiversity conservation,
- Clean transportation,
- Sustainable water and wastewater management,
- Climate change adapted products, production technologies and processes,
- Green buildings (International Capital Market Association, 2021a).

The first green bond, a Climate Awareness Bond, was issued in 2007 by the European Investment Bank. Since then, the green bond market has been expanding rapidly. In 2020, $269.5 billion were issued worldwide, compared to $104 billion in 2015. The cumulative issuance in 2020 surpassed $1 trillion (Climate Bonds Initiative, 2021b). The U.S. was the largest in national rankings at over $50 billion, followed by Germany, France, and China. The largest institutional investor was Federal National Mortgage Association (Fannie Mae). Several rail transport operators were prominent issuers, including the New York Metropolitan Transportation Authority, Los Angeles County Metropolitan Transportation, San Francisco Bay Area Rapid Transit District, France's national railway operator SNCF and Japan's fast train network operator JRRT (Ibid.). Other large U.S. issues include the Power Authority of the State of New York, Florida Development Finance Corporation, Illinois Finance Authority, San Francisco Public Utilities, San Diego County Water Authority, and Los Angeles County Public Works (Nastu, 2021). Some experts believe that green bonds are currently more limited by supply rather than demand (National Academies of Sciences, Engineering, and Medicine [National Academies], 2021, p. 15). If so, this market will continue to grow for the foreseeable future.

Social bonds raise funds for projects with positive social outcomes. Sustainability bonds are bonds where the proceeds will be exclusively used to finance a combination of green and social projects. Sustainability bonds follow the Sustainable Bond Guidelines (SBG), also established by the International Capital Market Association. These guidelines use the same four components for green bonds listed above (International Capital Market Association, 2021b). The first U.S. tax-exempt sustainability bonds were issued by the Massachusetts Bay Transportation Authority in 2017 (see case discussion below).

5.3.2 Experience with Green, Social and Sustainable (GSS) Bonds

GSS bonds are attractive to both investors and issuers. Investors may wish to invest in projects that fund environmental and social projects. They may also believe that GSS bonds signal lower environmental, social, and governance risk and therefore indicate stronger management and higher long-run returns. Or they may simply be interested in broadening their portfolios (National Academies, 2021, pp. 7–8).

Issuers are attracted to GSS bonds because they improve their reputation for environmental sustainability and perhaps their environmental performance. Since 2013, the Climate Bonds Initiative has issued a Climate Bonds Taxonomy that identifies projects across eight industries that reduce carbon initiatives. The projects fall into one of four categories: automatically qualified, potentially qualified pending meeting other criteria, not qualified, and more information needed (Climate Bonds Initiative, 2021a). Bond issues that automatically qualify likely entail less expense for issuers to bring them to market and generate more interest from investors.

There is no consistent evidence that green bonds carry a premium. There is research on both sides of the issue. "This is not surprising; given that financial markets are incredibly dynamic, no two bonds are identical, and the definition of green is highly variable, it is exceedingly difficult to obtain sufficient data to quantitatively demonstrate a pricing benefit for green bonds" (National Academies, 2021, p. 14).

The main weakness of GSS bonds is the additional monitoring and reporting costs. These costs may be one-time costs to develop the government's sustainability goals and to link specific projects with these goals. They may also include process development, prospectus development, and establishing a tracking system to ensure that bond proceeds are spent on the designated projects. "After the initial cost of developing organizational capacity to issue green bonds … preparing the required disclosures to issue green bonds cost about $10,000 in staff time" (National Academies, 2021, p. 1). While this is not a large amount for a large issuance, it can be prohibitive for smaller debt issues.

Another concern with green bonds is what is known as "greenwashing," which involves misleading potential investors about the environmental impacts of the project. These allegations can damage the issuer's reputation, potentially for the long term. This underscores the importance of following the components of green bonds, providing truthful disclosures and regular annual reports.

One important nuance for GSS municipal bonds is their tax-exempt status. In general, this is attractive to U.S. taxpayers and leads to lower interest rates for municipal bonds. However, the tax advantage is not of importance to international investors, who are less likely to be interested in tax-free bonds because of their low return and inability to enjoy the tax benefit. Instead, a municipality considering a GSS bond may want to consider a taxable issuance which may attract a wider pool of international investors (National Academies, 2021, p. 18).

5.3.3 Green Bonds for Sewer and Stormwater Repair Projects

The City of Saint Paul, Minnesota, issued Minnesota's first green bond in 2015 and became one of the first green bond issuers in the nation. The city owns and maintains 804 miles of sanitary sewers and 450 miles of storm sewers. Most of the city's sanitary sewers are at least 50 years old, and many are 75–125 years old, so there was a long-term need for improvements. The proceeds from the green bonds were spent on sewer repairs, stormwater quality improvements, and the rehabilitation of sewers and tunnels.

The city had traditionally used tax-exempt municipal bonds to fund capital projects for the city. The sewer utility's capital projects clearly have an environmental impact. The city committed to make sustainability and green initiatives a priority, so green bonds were a logical option. The city began to explore the potential issuance of green bonds as part of its annual infrastructure debt financing program in late 2014 (City of Saint Paul, Office of Financial Services, 2016). By working with the city's financial advisor, the green bond designation was applied to the sewer revenue bond. In 2015, the city's $8.7 million Sewer Revenue Green Bonds were the first sold in Minnesota. And since then, the city has issued green bonds every year for sewer projects (City of Saint Paul, Office of Financial Services, 2020). These bonds are secured solely by revenues of the city's sewer utility.

The city established formal processes to ensure that the program complies with the four components of the GBP: the proper categorization and use of proceeds, project evaluation and selection, management of proceeds, and reporting. The green bond reports are posted on the city's website and provide potential investors information regarding the projects financed and their environmental impact. A detailed listing of the specific projects is available in the annual report.

The city seeks to be a leader in sustainability and is now focusing on carbon dioxide reduction activities such as "energy efficiency and conservation, clean energy supply, alternative fuels and transportation options, recycling and waste reduction, urban reforestation and natural resources management, and water resources management" (City of Saint Paul, Office of Financial Services, 2016). The city adopted a "Climate Action and Resilience Plan" in December 2019, which has the goal of achieving carbon neutrality in city operations by 2030. As such, green bonds are an important tool for the city to meet the financing goals of repairing infrastructure and meet environmental policy goals.

Lessons Learned: It is important to ensure compliance with the four components of the GBP and to regularly provide a report for current and potential investors. The city's green bond report format is similar from one year to the next, so after the first year, it was mostly a matter of updating the report. It was also important initially that the city worked with municipal financing experts to identify and comply with the best practices of a green bond sale. Subsequent sales followed a similar pattern, so it did not take as much staff time after the first time.

It is important that the city had a long-term commitment to environmental and climate action policies over different Mayoral administrations, as this allowed for consistency in policy, which is important to investors.

5.3.4 Sustainability Bonds for Transit Projects

Projects: In 2017, the Massachusetts Bay Transportation Authority (MBTA) issued $99 million of sustainability bonds, the first tax-exempt sustainability bonds issued in the U.S. "Before issuance, the MBTA formed an internal Sustainability Committee made up of internal stakeholders, directors, and managers to lead the drafting of the Sustainability Bond Framework" (National Academies, 2021). The Framework used the Sustainability Bond Guidelines of the International Capital Management Association. Projects fit into either the environmental (green bonds) category or the social bond category:

Environment

- Built environment: Respecting, protecting, and improving the built environment and enhancing the quality of the travel experience.
- Capacity: Reducing emissions from personal vehicle trips by increasing capacity to carry passengers and increasing the attractiveness of public transit by offering more frequent, reliable, and comfortable service.
- Carbon, energy, and climate resilience: Reducing carbon emissions and preparing for the potential impacts of climate change and extreme weather.
- Natural environment: Respecting, protecting, and enhancing the natural environment and its contribution to the quality of life.
- Noise: Managing and controlling transport-related noise and vibration.
- Pollution prevention: Proactively managing activities to minimize and control pollution.
- Resource management: Using resources wisely and minimizing waste.

Social

- Affordability: Balancing customers' means, particularly low-income riders, with the organization's financial constraints.
- Accessibility: Operating an inclusive system with facilities designed to accommodate a diverse customer base.
- Availability: Ensuring that communities within the service area have reasonable, equitable access to the system.
- Equity: Offsetting social and environmental burdens experienced by populations or communities within the service area and/or striving for an even distribution of benefits and burdens across the diverse modes, customer bases, and service area.
- Safety: Protecting the well-being of passengers, operators, and the general public.
- Workplace environment: Maintaining a safe, empowering, and satisfying workplace environment for MBTA and affiliated employees (MBTA, 2018, p. 5).

The committee included representatives from several MBTA departments and sought the advice of external stakeholders. The committee selected projects from the MBTA's capital improvement program using a project selection process guided by the Framework. The project funded over 100 projects ranging in cost from \$100,000 to \$9.8 million for projects addressing priorities such as climate resiliency, rider capacity, pollution prevention, and accessibility. The MBTA publishes an annual Sustainability Bond Progress Report.

Lessons Learned: The bonds were more favorably received by the market than a traditional MBTA bond offering at the same time. "In fact, six of the eight banks that participated in both offerings submitted more aggressive bids on the sustainability bond... This increased demand translated into a lifetime interest savings of approximately \$2.60 per \$1,000 issued" (National Academies, 2021, p. 25). The bond was recognized as *The Bond Buyer*'s 2017 Northeast Regional Deal of the Year and a finalist for the National Deal of the Year award.

As the first such offering, it was important that the MBTA did careful up-front work to ensure the projects met the Sustainability Bond Guidelines, ensuring investors that the funds would indeed be used for projects meeting the Guidelines. This established that sustainability bonds could address social and environmental benefits, and that there is a demand by investors for sustainable bonds. In the spring of 2020, the MBTA issued its second sustainability bond for \$45.7 million for more than 50 projects.

5.4 Public-Private Partnerships (P3s)

5.4.1 Description

In the U.S., the growing demands for upgrading and expanding public infrastructure systems and constraints on public resources have led to calls for more private investment in public infrastructure. Public-Private Partnerships (PPPs, or P3s) are commonly defined as a contractual arrangement in which governments form partnerships with the private sector to design, finance, build, operate, and maintain infrastructures such as toll roads, water supply facilities, and wastewater treatment plants (US DOT, 2012). Building on a contractual agreement, the resources, assets, and skills of public and private sectors are shared in delivering a facility for the use of the general public. Moreover, through this agreement, each sector shares in the risks and rewards potential in the delivery of the facility.

Many different types of P3s exist. They are often characterized by dividing the responsibility for the five major functions of project development (design, build, operate, maintain, and finance) between the government and the private entity. Yescombe (2012) identifies the key characteristics of P3s as:

- A long-term contract between the public and private organizations.
- Private assumption of one or more of the responsibilities and risks of designing, building, operating, maintaining, and financing a project.
- Reimbursement of the private party by the public agency for the investment and risk of the project.
- Ownership of the facility remaining with the government or, as agreed upon, being transferred at a specified time.

P3s are not new to the U.S.; however, they are used less in the U.S. compared with other countries such as the U.K. and Australia. One main reason for the limited growth of P3s in the U.S. is due to the unique tax-exempt municipal bond market, which allows state and local governments to borrow at lower costs in the private capital market (US CBO, 2020). In recent years, due to the increasing gap between infrastructure demands and available public funding, there has been a growing interest in P3s. As of August 2018, 36 states had authorized P3-enabling legislation. In a 2016 survey by the ICMA (2017), 119 of 601 governments (19.8%) responded that they actively used P3s. Typically, those governments that utilized P3s tended to be larger, perhaps because the complexity of P3s requires a high degree of expertise. The resources to learn about the benefits of and the challenges to P3 have grown rapidly.

5.4.2 Portland Transit Extension

Project: A P3 was used to build an extension of the Metropolitan Area Express (MAX) light rail line to link the urban core of Portland to the Portland International Airport (PDX). Three other transit stations were part of the project. The MAX system is operated by TriMet, a public agency that provides bus and rail transit in the Portland metropolitan area, and PDX is operated by the Port of Portland. TriMet and PDX joined with the Portland Development Commission (an independent city economic development authority) to agree to a P3 with Bechtel Enterprises.

Bechtel provided funding for 23.1% of the project's $128.8 million construction and engineering costs and received a sole-source, no-bid contract to design and build the extension. In return, Bechtel received the right to develop a mixed-use development near the new MAX station. The development included office space, retail, hotels, and a gas station. The three public agencies paid for the remainder of the rail link construction and engineering costs. Transit fares partially offset operating costs. No federal funds were used. The project was completed more than 10 years earlier than had been planned. It is estimated that the public costs to develop the extension were reduced by about 23% by the P3 (Gosling & Freeman, 2012, p. 11). The extension improved transit access to the airport and encouraged greater use of transit for airport trips. This example demonstrates how a project can leverage values in ways that could not be done without a private sector partner. Private developers can use new transit stops for retail, office, or commercial development and often extract more value than public agencies typically can. Public agencies benefit from completing the projects faster and at a lower cost. In this case, the improved airport access was an additional benefit for the region. It required the city to agree to waive bidding requirements and a sole-source contract with Bechtel. Public participation did not occur until after the negotiation and design, and so was less influential. A high level of trust between the partners was important.

Lessons Learned: P3s are not a panacea to address infrastructure challenges, but their ability to leverage private sector capital and expertise can help governments confront complex challenges and accelerate project completion. However, building a successful partnership between the public and private sectors is inherently challenging. It is important to balance the profit goal of private companies with the public interest and create a win-win for both parties. A successful P3 should allow the public sector to advance public value and allow the private party to secure its required return. Maintaining a high level of trust between the partners is crucial to implement P3s. To further protect public interests in P3s, engaging political leaders and the general public in the early project development stage is recommended, though not necessary as demonstrated in the Portland case.

5.5 Privatization

5.5.1 Description

Compared to Public-Private Partnerships (P3s), privatization is further along the continuum away from publicly provided services. As discussed above and in the previous chapter, P3s include several arrangements involving private participation in the five key phases of designing, building, operating, finance, and maintaining a facility. Privatization involves greater private participation in these phases. For example, in building a *new public facility*, some possible privatization arrangements include:

- Design-Build-Operate-Transfer (DBOT): The firm designs and builds a new facility, operates it for an agreed upon time, then transfers it to the government. Financing may be public, private, or shared.
- Design-Build-Own-Operate (DBOO): Like DBOT, except the firm owns the facility under a long-term contract or franchise agreement and assumes the risk and keeps the profit (Savas, 2000, pp. 244–247).

In the situation where an *existing public facility* is rehabilitated or expanded, the firm may lease or buy the facility from the government, then operate it and collect user fees under a concession agreement for a specified time. Typically, the level and rate of increase of the user fees are specified in the agreement, as is the level of service and/or maintenance spending.

The key distinction between P3s and privatization is that the private partner assumes partial or full ownership of the facility. While it is common for private investors or individuals to hold bonds backing an infrastructure project, this is not the same as holding equity which entitles investors to profits after the costs and required reserves are paid. "Under the municipal bond model, the private sector has one concern – full and timely payment of bonds. Under the private equity model, the private sector hopes that revenue will exceed forecasts and yield returns greater than expected" (Ortiz & Buxbaum, 2008, p. 136).

One of the key concerns of private firms in these situations is risk. There are many dimensions of risk in these situations. Costs of construction or operation may be higher than expected for many reasons, and revenues may be less either because of lower-than-expected demand, competition, or contractual restrictions on raising fees. There may also be environmental/regulatory risk caused by unexpected environmental damage leading to regulations affecting the firm's profits. Changes in technology may also affect a long-term project (Page et al., 2008; Savas, 2000). The higher the risk for the firm, the less attractive the investment, and they will want to push these risks back on to the government or the public. In some cases, governments can assume risks more easily than firms because they control factors such as regulation and user fees. When the government can assume this risk, it can lead to favorable conditions for a mutually beneficial agreement.

The longer the agreement term, the lower the risk for the concessionaire, especially if they can structure the debt in a favorable way. Long-term investments in U.S. infrastructure are particularly attractive to some investors, such as pension funds and endowments, because these investments have a similar long-term focus with an emphasis on stable returns. In addition, some concession agreements such as toll roads may have inflation escalation clauses which provide effective hedges against inflation, which is also attractive to long-term investors (Page et al., 2008).

Broadly speaking, Donahue (1989 pp. 79–80, emphasis original) articulates the conditions when privatization can be preferred to public provision: "*The more precisely a task can be specified in advance and its performance evaluated after the fact, the more certainly contractors can be made to compete; the more readily disappointing contractors can be replaced (or otherwise penalized); and the more narrowly government cares about ends to the exclusion of means, the stronger becomes the case for employing profit-seekers rather than civil servants.*"

The strengths of privatization then include:

- access to private sector expertise and skills,
- typically, faster construction of new facilities,
- transfer of risk to the party who can most easily bear it, and
- up-front payment to the government.

The weaknesses include:

- complicated contracts and negotiations,

- enforcement and monitoring costs, and
- loss of public control and flexibility.

5.5.2 Chicago Skyway and Indiana East–West Toll Road

Projects: The City of Chicago, Illinois pioneered the privatization of municipal infrastructure with the first long-term lease of an existing toll road in the US. In 2005, the city leased the Chicago Skyway, a 7.8-mile city-owned toll road, for 99 years for $1.83 billion to the Skyway Concession Company, owned by Cintra Macquarie, a consortium of Australian and Spanish private investors. The city initially hoped to receive about $900 million, so the actual amount was a huge windfall. The city was able to pay off the outstanding bonds, which led to an upgrading of their credit rating (Ashton et al., 2020). More than half of the traffic on the Skyway comes from out-of-state drivers, reducing the political opposition. While competing routes are congested, the Skyway is not.

The Skyway Concession Company is responsible for operating and maintenance costs and collecting toll revenues. Their business approach is to combine geographically diverse investments into portfolios that can then be packaged and sold to investors. They were able to refinance their short-term variable rate debt with long-term bonds, lowering their risk and increasing the value of these assets. "This generated a $373 million windfall that it paid out as a distribution to equity investors [which] helped Macquarie generate a 21% internal rate of return for the investors" (Ashton et al., 2020, p. 2).

In 2006, Cintra Macquarie, doing business as Indiana Toll Road Concession Company (ITRCC), also leased the 156-mile Indiana East–West Toll Road for $3.85 billion for 75 years, about twice as much as anticipated. The Toll Road flows directly into the Chicago Skyway, and so is the main source of Skyway traffic. The ITRCC filed for bankruptcy in 2014, but other Australian investors bought the concession and exited bankruptcy in 2015 (Renn, 2016). Like the Chicago Skyway, most of the traffic on the East–West Toll Road comes from out-of-state drivers, reducing the political opposition. Some of the funds received by the State of Indiana were used for infrastructure aid in the area and other parts of the state, as well as rehabilitating bridges and pavement throughout the state. This also helped generate political support for the deal.

Lessons Learned: These investments were more attractive than expected. This was for several reasons:

- These toll roads provided a predictable cash flow and did not face the high up-front costs and revenue risks faced by a new project.
- U.S. governments are generally stable investments with a reliable legal system that enforces contracts (Ortiz & Buxbaum, 2008). This makes them attractive to international investors.
- Equity investment opportunities in infrastructure attract a new set of investors, "with higher tolerances for risk, which in turn tend to generate more liberal appraisals of asset value" (Garvin & Bosso, 2008, p. 164).

This helps to explain the higher-than-expected sales prices for the Chicago Skyway and the East-West Toll Road, which brought huge windfalls to both governments. These funds can then be used for other important public infrastructure projects. In both cases, most of the tolls are paid by non-residents, reducing political opposition. The proceeds of the sales were also used well politically.

The Skyway was a nonessential service appropriate for privatization because the focus was not on the means of service delivery, but the ends, as opposed to a core municipal service where government cares about both the means and ends.

While this was a successful case, there are some downsides to these sorts of arrangements:

- Long-term leases constrain future options for the government. Many things can change, including technology, demand for goods, political preferences, and desirable performance standards, and it is difficult to anticipate future citizen demands.
- Concessionaires "may cut costs by taking actions that harm a vulnerable segment of society, such as low-income citizens" (Chicago Council on Global Affairs, 2011).
- Long-term leases shift revenues from the future into the present. While this may be good in some cases, in other cases, it may transfer wealth from future generations to current citizens.

5.5.3 Parking Meters in Chicago

Project: In 2008, the City of Chicago, led by Mayor Richard M. Daley, leased its 36,000 on-street meters for 75 years to a Morgan Stanley-led investment group for $1.16 billion. Only one other qualified vendor submitted a bid. The concessionaire was required to install kiosks for payments to accept credit cards and was given a non-compete clause that prohibited the city from opening off-street parking lots that would compete with the meters. The use of the funds undermined public opinion. Initially, the proceeds were to be used for reserve funds to replace the $17 million in annual lost parking meter revenues and a "human infrastructure" fund for community economic development projects. Instead, the payment was largely used to cover the city's budget deficits due to the Great Recession. Further, the city was required to reimburse the concessionaire for revenue lost due to street closures, street festivals, parking waivers for the disabled, and public works projects interrupting the flow of meter revenue. The city was billed $55 million in the first two years for these events, and this provision required the city to repurchase rights-of-way for bike lanes, bus rapid transit lanes, or other elements of their sustainability action plan (Ashton et al., 2020). "By 2010, only $180 million was left" of the $1.16 billion (Renn, 2016, p. 6).

In most Chicago neighborhoods, parking meter rates increased from 25 cents per hour to $2 an hour. Downtown parking meter rates increased from $3.50 in 2009 to $6.50 an hour by 2013. "The higher rates provoked outrage. Meters broke as they overflowed with quarters before the new credit card-reading kiosks were installed" (Renn, 2016, p. 6). The city was required to take harsh measures against drivers not paying their parking fees with "boot" vehicle clamps and license suspensions which were said to have a "disproportionate impact on low-income and minority divers, many of whom ended up in bankruptcy owing to their inability to pay" (Ashtonet al., 2020, p. 3). In 2008, incoming Mayor Rahm Emanuel said "This was a bad deal for our city and a bad contract for our residents. They city should never have done this deal. Period" (Renn, 2016, p. 4).

Lessons Learned: Mayor Daley gave the city council only three days to vote on the agreement, and it was approved after one hour of debate by a 40–5 vote. Some council members later admitted that they did not have time to review the agreement. "The Chicago inspector general noted that very limited financial information was provided to the council. No financial analysis of the parking meter system's value was provided. No public comment or expert testimony was given, nor was there any presentation of comparable studies or alternative lease terms" (Calia & Msall, 2011 p. 12). "The rushed approval process created a public perception that the parking meter deal was illegitimate, if not crooked" (Renn, 2016, p. 8). Complicated agreements like this that affect a wide variety of citizens need to be explained and perhaps adapted to achieve consensus and legitimacy.

The financial outcome for the city was a major loss. The funds were not used as planned, and the city lost the revenue stream from meters as the concessionaire was entitled to all of it. The city receives only $2.5 million annually from the reserve fund created with the proceeds of the sale, as opposed to $17 million in meter revenue prior to the agreement. Perhaps the worst part of the agreement for the city was the requirement to reimburse the concessionaire for meter closures in excess of an annual allowance. "Compensation payments for free disabled parking alone reached as much as $21 million per year" (Renn, 2016, p. 10). The Emanuel administration renegotiated this payment down to $6.5 million annually, but this obligation, combined with the lost annual meter revenue, made this a net loss of $35 million for the city. This budget gap will last for the 75 years of the lease.

Parking spaces are not highly "asset-specific"—that is, unlike toll roads that can only be used for one thing, parking spaces can be used for other uses other than parking, and increasingly are—for bus rapid transit lanes, cycling lanes, or converted back to sidewalks. Thus, a long-term agreement that dedicates this land for parking locks the government into using this land in this way for many years. The same is true of similarly flexible urban spaces such as sidewalks and green spaces. Further, the city tied itself into a narrow contract by not being able to provide free or discounted parking to the disabled or any other groups to whom they might want to provide a discount: carpools, busses, or school vans.

5.6 Crowdfunding

5.6.1 Description

Crowdfunding is the sourcing of small amounts of funds from a large group of individuals. It is an emerging method and has become increasingly popular for raising donations for a wide variety of projects. Crowdfunding builds a connection between entrepreneurs who aim at raising the fund (the fundraisers) and the investors (the crowd) who are willing to invest small amounts through an internet-based intermediary (an online platform).

Civic crowdfunding has been successful in funding small municipal infrastructure projects. An estimated $50 million has been raised by 2019 (Gasparro, 2019). More than 60% of civic crowdfunding campaigns by 2015 had successfully reached or exceeded their target amount (Gasparro, 2015).

There are several popular online platforms for civic crowdfunding: ioby, Spacehive, neighbor.ly.[1] While civic crowdfunding can be used for any project, Gasparro (2015, p. 6) believes that it "has huge potential to be used for municipal infrastructure projects." Civic crowdfunding is not only a potential source of funding but also a way to gauge civic demand for a project by seeing the response to the crowdfunding appeal. It also typically is more decentralized than the typical state or local decision-making process, as the group of people (who may or may not be citizens of the jurisdiction) can raise funds for a project without having to go through the often slow and cumbersome process of attaining approval and appropriation by a governing body and ensuring the funds are spent on the desired project. Further, other citizens who may not want to pay their tax dollars for the project do not have to. Thus "niche projects" that appeal to relatively small groups but not the government's broader citizenry can be funded without taxing other citizens.

It is uncommon for civic crowdfunding to supply all the necessary funds for a project. One common approach is for crowdfunding to provide "first dollar" funding. For example, if a city is unsure about the demand for a project, an appeal on a crowdfunding platform can establish whether there is sufficient demand by seeing if the minimum level of funding is achieved. If so, other public funding sources are made available; if not, the project is not approved, and the funds are returned. This can lower the perceived risk to other investors by enduring sufficient demand before committing to the project. "Last dollar" or "last mile" funding calls for support after an initial decision has been made but before the public funds are released. They may also be for enhancements to the project or to enable the project to be implemented faster.

Crowdfunding initially employed a "patronage model" where contributions to the project were seen as an opportunity for people to donate without expecting a return. In the case of the "rewards-based model," funders receive a nonfinancial reward, often a small gift for their donation. New models are emerging in situations where the project will generate a revenue stream in the future. The "lending model" is like a bank loan, where the funders receive a fixed return. One example is the use of community bonds by the Center for Social Innovation in Canada. The Center has issued bonds backed by mortgages for buildings that they purchased or restored for the use of nonprofit organizations, and the investors have a claim to these mortgages, providing a return on their investment (Young, 2017). Another model is the "investor

[1] Neighborly was created in 2012. It was an online crowdfunding platform specifically focused on raising money for critical fiber broadband infrastructure to communities. However, it was shuttered after failing to secure funding in 2019.

model," where investors acquire an equity position in the project and receive a variable return like a stock dividend. The Securities and Exchange Commission now allows crowdfunding platforms to bypass securities brokers, making the investor model easier (Young 2017). Some platforms provide detailed information so potential investors and lenders can make informed decisions, reducing their risk and improving the likelihood of investment.

5.6.2 Experience with Crowdfunding

Research on civic crowdfunding has found that projects that meet their funding goal are more likely to do so quickly and tend to attract the support of a group or local businesses (Gasparro, 2015). Projects are also more likely to be approved and to fund a higher percentage if the request is smaller (Mayer, 2019). More recently, government involvement has been found to provide a "certification" that verifies that the funding will be used as promised, increasing the citizen's trust in a project (Hong & Ryu, 2019). In South Korea, a law passed in 2015 created a process where a government agency would review crowdfunding proposals, select those deemed feasible, and then provide this information on the crowdsourcing platform to potential funders. Examining 110 projects on the Korean crowdfunding platform Wadiz in 2016, Hong and Ryu (2019) found that government support for a project increased the success in achieving project funding goal by 64% and increased the amount funded by 55%. This suggests that, properly done, there is a positive synergy between the momentum of a crowd and the stability provided by government assurance. This is like traditional private investing, where government bond guarantees improve the return on bonds, and some degree of stock market regulation improves investor confidence.

An example of the positive synergy between crowdfunding and government participation is a small project in the City of Nephi, Utah, population of 5,560. Nephi had a baseball field without lights. The city approached several foundations for contributions to install lights. The foundations were willing to help but wanted to see some local effort. A crowdfunding request was made on Rockethub. The city publicized the fundraising effort through traditional media, which attracted other donors, some of whom were less comfortable giving through crowdfunding , or wanted to be recognized for their donation. This provided more assurance about the viability of the project. In the end, the funding came from three sources: five foundations provided a total of $112,500, and direct donations and crowdfunding from both businesses and individuals provided $12,500. There were no legal barriers and no restrictions. The City Administrator said the project presented little risk. In this case and many others, crowdfunding is complemented by other sources. Indeed, the publicity created by crowdfunding often helps leverage other donations as well as government funding. The few legal barriers and restrictions make it easier to raise funds this way, and the risk can be minimal.

The strengths of civic crowdfunding as a means of funding infrastructure include:

- Reduced capital costs associated with privately financed infrastructure.
- Able to fund small infrastructure projects quickly with less government funding.
- Reduces the risk to investors because it can ensure there is sufficient demand before the investors commit funds to the project.
- Involvement of local citizens and other funders in a decentralized, voluntary way.

The weaknesses of civic crowdfunding in funding infrastructure include:

- Difficultly in funding large infrastructure projects.
- Effort required to initiate a funding campaign.
- Risk of online platform closure and failure or loss of reputation if funds are not returned.

5.6.3 Crowdfunding for a Recreation Project

Project: The City of Culver, Oregon (population 1,442) was approached by the family, friends, and the "church family" of a child who passed away to honor his memory by building a splash pad in a park. The city told the group that if they raised the funds, the city would provide the land and assume the ownership responsibility and costs for the splash pad. The group used a crowdfunding approach to raise funds through gofundme.com. In addition to this source, there were bake sales at the school, and the Rotary Club made this project their fundraising event for the year. In total, these groups raised about $33,000. This project caught the attention of a pool company that donated the splash pad.

The group raised funds and worked with the city to authorize payment of bills related to the project. There were no legal barriers or restrictions to using this tool. The impetus came from the family, community, and the church, and the funds were raised very quickly, so within a year, the project went from an idea to a reality. The operating costs have been high, and the city was not prepared to take on this expense. Also, the city needed to decide how to pay the costs of maintenance and replacement in the future.

Lessons Learned: The city did not initiate the project and did not incur any out-of-pocket expenses initially. The city did provide the land and incurred maintenance and operating costs after the project was completed. Thus, there was no risk and no cost to taxpayers initially, but there has been since then. The energy of the community groups was important in publicizing the project and raising funds. The City Manager referred to it as an "emotion-driven project," a good illustration of a niche project. Also, the rapid success of this small project fits with the research findings mentioned: that projects that meet their funding goal are more likely to do so quickly, are also that smaller projects are more likely to be approved and to fund a higher percentage.

5.6.4 Crowdfunding for Cycling

Projects: In 2014, the City of Memphis, Tennessee, issued a crowdfunding campaign to help build a local bike transportation project. This was the first American bike transportation project paid for in part by crowdfunding. The organization Livable Memphis promoted an effort to enhance bicycling infrastructure. The Hampline project connected Binghampton, a low-income neighborhood, to the downtown and the bike path network. Total costs for this project were $2 million from public and private sources, and crowdfunding provided last-mile funding of $75,000 (compared to a $67,150 goal) through the platform ioby.org from approximately 500 donors. Donor names were inscribed on a plaque, and a bike rack and bike repair station were provided with the funds raised. Crowdfunding allowed Livable Memphis to vet the project and design plans, reducing the risk to donors. (City of Memphis Bikeway and Pedestrian Program, 2021; Gasparro, 2015).

In 2014, Denver, Colorado raised $36,085 of a $35,000 goal through ioby.org for the Arapahoe protected bike lane project from 250 individual and small businesses, 75% of whom were within 5 miles of the project (Gasparro, 2019). The campaign provided last-mile funding to fund the remaining amount needed to complete the project. The Downtown Denver Partnership (DDP) and City and County of Denver sought to create more protected bike lanes to accommodate a 42% increase in bike commuting. DDP secured $120,000 from the Gates Family Foundation and the Downtown Denver Business Improvement District (BID) (Gasparro, 2015). The

City pledged to cover half of the $70,000 of the design fees and the construction costs if the DDP could raise the other half of the design fees ($35,000). The project went from design to ribbon cutting in less than one year.

"DDP saw crowdfunding as an opportunity to allow community members and businesses to make a statement about what matters to them and to have the chance to 'vote with their dollars.' The ultimate goal of this campaign was to gain community buy-in" (Gasparro, 2015). "Letting communities vote with their dollars isn't just about budgets. It is much more about letting local residents and businesses know early on about the project and allowing them to participate in a meaningful way" (Gasparro, 2019). This shows how crowdfunding can be a more direct, decentralized way for citizens to express their preferences and reduce the risk of projects to the city and private civic groups.

"Instead of holding a short public comment period, community organizations engaged residents and business owners early in the design process. This made a huge difference" (Gasparro, 2019). The DDP gathered input about the project's design and worked with city planners to redesign the project in response to concerns about parking, access routes, and Fire Department access to hydrants. This helped attain buy-in to the project from those affected.

Despite this, some were frustrated by the crowdfunding approach to raising funds. A crowd funder in the project said, "It is NOT the community's responsibility to pay for infrastructure in any way beyond taxes ... The city needs to step up and pay for something that is good for the community and stop treating bike riding as a niche hobby" (Emphasis original, Gasparro, 2018). In addition, a member of the BID said that crowdfunding "is not a regular funding approach, that this is a one-time or limited use approach. I think it is fine to do it a couple of times but for various strategic reasons" (Gasparro, 2018).

Lessons Learned: In both cases, the amount raised was relatively small, but the funds were raised quickly, again consistent with research findings. Crowdfunding provided a meaningful opportunity for citizens to "vote with their dollars" and make their preferences known directly. Civic participation in crowdfunding and the discussion of the projects encouraged those involved to reach a consensus regarding design issues that might have created problems otherwise. However, the frustrations expressed suggest that at least in the Arapahoe Project, some participants do not see crowdfunding as a financing approach that should be used regularly for infrastructure projects.

References

Ashton, P., Doussard, M., & Weber, R. (2020, November 24). Sale of the century: Chicago's infrastructure deals and the privatization state. *Metropolitics*. https://metropolitics.org/Sale-of-the-Century-Chicago-s-Infrastructure-Deals-and-the-Privatization-State.html. Accessed 27 September 2021.

Calia, R., & Msall, L. (2011). The Chicago experience: A P3 checklist. *Government Finance Review, 27*(3), 8–13.

Chen, C. (2016). Banking on infrastructure: Exploring the fiscal impacts of state infrastructure bank (SIB) loans on leveraging state and local transportation investment. *Public Budgeting & Finance, 36*(3), 94–113.

Chicago Council on Global Affairs. (2011). The pros and cons of privatization. *Government Finance Review, 27*(3), 14–20.

City and County of Denver website. (2016). *Mayor Hancock announces social impact bonds to serve first 25 participants at North Colorado*. https://www.denvergov.org/content/denvergov/en/mayors-office/newsroom/2016/mayor-hancock-announces-social-impact-bonds-to-serve-first-25-pa.html. Accessed 27 September 2021.

City of Memphis Bikeway and Pedestrian Program. (2021). *The Hampline*. https://bikepedmemphis.wordpress.com/projects-2/hampline/. Accessed 27 September 2021.

City of Saint Paul, Office of Financial Services. (2016). *Series 2015B sewer revenue green bond report*. https://www.stpaulbonds.com/city-of-saint-paul-minnesota-mn/additional-info/i565?i=1. Accessed 27 September 2021.

City of Saint Paul, Office of Financial Services. (2020). *2020 green bonds report for the city of Saint Paul*. https://www.stpaulbonds.com/city-of-saint-paul-minnesota-mn/additional-info/i565?i=1. Accessed 27 September 2021.

Climate Bonds Initiative. (2021a). *Climate bonds taxonomy*. https://www.climatebonds.net/files/files/CBI_Taxonomy_Tables-2June21.pdf. Accessed 27 September 2021.

Climate Bonds Initiative. (2021b). *Record $269.5 billion green issuance for 2020: Late surge sees pandemic year pip 2019 total by $3 billion*. https://www.climatebonds.net/2021/01/record-2695bn-green-issuance-2020-late-surge-sees-pandemic-year-pip-2019-total-3bn. Accessed 27 September 2021.

Donahue, J. D. (1989). *The privatization decision: Public ends, private means*. Basic Books.

Garvin, M. J., & Bosso, D. (2008). Assessing the effectiveness of infrastructure public-private partnership programs and projects. *Public Works Management & Policy, 13*(2), 162–178.

Gasparro, K. (2015). *Funding municipal infrastructure: Integrating project finance and crowdfunding*. https://gpc.stanford.edu/sites/default/files/wp87.pdf. Accessed 27 September 2021.

Gasparro, K. (2018). A tale of two bike lanes. In P. G. Coy (Ed.), *Research in social movements, conflicts and change* (pp. 39–62). Emerald Publishing.

Gasparro, K. (2019). Civic crowdfunding reduces the risk of 'Bikelash'. *The Conversation.* https://theconversation.com/civic-crowdfunding-reduces-the-risk-of-bikelash-114049. Accessed 27 September 2021.

Gosling, G. D., & Freeman, D. (2012). *Case study report: Portland max airport extension. Research Project 2503* (Mineta Transportation Institute Working Paper). San Jose State University. https://transweb.sjsu.edu/sites/default/files/pdfs/research/2503-cs6-Portland-MAX-Airport-Extension.pdf. Accessed 27 September 2021.

Hong, S., & Ryu, J. (2019). Crowdfunding public projects: Collaborative governance for achieving citizen co-funding of public goods. *Government Information Quarterly, 36*(1), 145–153.

International Capital Market Association. (2021a). *Green bond principles: Voluntary process guidelines for issuing green bonds.* https://www.icmagroup.org/assets/documents/Sustainable-finance/2021-updates/Green-Bond-Principles-June-2021-140621.pdf. Accessed 27 September 2021.

International Capital Market Association. (2021b). *Sustainability bond guidelines.* https://www.icmagroup.org/assets/documents/Sustainable-finance/2021-updates/Sustainability-Bond-Guidelines-June-2021-140621.pdf. Accessed 27 September 2021.

International City/County Management Association (ICMA). (2017). *Innovations and emerging practices in local government 2016 survey: Summary report of results.* https://icma.org/sites/default/files/309068_ICMA%20Innovation%20Survey%20Summary%20Report.pdf. Accessed 1 August 2021.

Massachusetts Bay Transportation Authority [MBTA]. (2018). *Sustainable bond progress report (2018).* https://cdn.mbta.com/sites/default/files/2018-12/2018-12-sustainability-bond-progress-report.pdf. Accessed 27 September 2021.

Mayer, M. (2019). An exploratory look at the growth and success of crowdfunding in the public space. *State and Local Government Review, 51*(3), 18–96.

National Academies of Sciences, Engineering and Medicine. (2021). *Analysis of green bond financing in the public transportation industry*. The National Academies Press.

Natsu, J. (2021). Municipal market embraces ESG and boosts green-labelled debt. *Environment + Energy Leader.* https://www.environmentalleader.com/2021/02/municipal-market-embraces-esg-boosts-green-labeled-debt/. Accessed 27 September 2021.

Ohio Department of Transportation. (2011). 2010 state infrastructure bank (SIB) annual report. https://www.transportation.ohio.gov/wps/portal/gov/odot/programs/state-infrastructure-bank/sib-reports/sib-report-2010. Accessed 20 January 2022.

Ohio DOT. (2021). *2020 state infrastructure bank (SIB) annual report*. https://www.transportation.ohio.gov/wps/portal/gov/odot/programs/state-infrastructure-bank/sib-reports/sib-report-2020. Accessed 2 September 2021.

Ortiz, I. N., & Buxbaum, J. N. (2008). Protecting the public interest in long-term concession agreements for transportation infrastructure. *Public Works Management & Policy, 13*(2), 126–137.

Page, S. N., Ankner, W., Jones, C., & Fetterman, R. (2008). The risks and rewards of private equity in infrastructure. *Public Works Management & Policy, 13*(2), 100–113.

Renaissance Planning Group. (2014). *Promoting joint development in Florida.* https://fdotwww.blob.core.windows.net/sitefinity/docs/default-source/content/transit/pages/jdtechmemofinal20140109.pdf?sfvrsn=5eb25c9_0. Accessed 2 September 2021.

Renn, A. M. (2016). *The lessons of long-term privatizations: Why Chicago got it wrong, and Indiana got it right.* Manhattan Institute. https://www.manhattan-institute.org/html/lessons-long-term-privatizations-chicago-indiana-9052.html. Accessed 27 September 2021.

Savas, E. S. (2000). *Privatization and public-private partnerships.* Chatham House Publishers.

Silva, E., Hernandez, A., & Linn, J. (2012). *Maximizing transit's potential with the urban centers of tomorrow.* http://www.sfrpc.com/TOD/citiesthatwork-289dd1/Documents/MeetingMaterials/140616/PPTPres_MDC_FAPA_2012_TOD_Presentation.pdf. Accessed 12 September 2021.

US Department of Transportation. (2012). *Risk assessment for public-private partnerships: A primer.* https://www.fhwa.dot.gov/ipd/pdfs/p3/p3_risk_assessment_primer_122612.PDF. Accessed 2 September 2021.

US Department of Transportation. (2019). *Value capture: Capitalizing on the value created by transportation.* https://www.fhwa.dot.gov/ipd/pdfs/value_capture/value_capture_implementation_manual_2019.pdf. Accessed 2 September 2021.

US CBO. (2020). *Public-private partnerships for transportation and water infrastructure.* https://www.cbo.gov/publication/56003. Accessed 27 September 2021.

Yescombe, E. R. (2012). Public-private partnerships. In J. R. Bartle, W. B. Hildreth, & J. Marlowe (Eds.), *Management policies in local government finance* (pp. 361–385). International City/County Management Association Press.

Young, D. R. (2017). *Financing nonprofits and other social enterprises: A benefits approach.* Edward Elgar Publishing.

Zhao, Z. J., Das, K. V., & Larson, K. (2012). Joint development as a value capture strategy for public transit finance. *Journal of Transport and Land Use, 5*(1), 5–17.

6

Conclusion: Putting Innovation into Practice

This chapter concludes the book. The first section summarizes the key findings of innovative infrastructure financing. The second section presents the challenges of using innovative infrastructure financing. The last section concludes and provides suggestions for the deployment of innovative infrastructure financing.

6.1 Findings

As discussed in Chapter 1, state and local governments across the U.S. have been facing a serious infrastructure deficit for several years. The share of state and local spending on infrastructure in 2017 was at the lowest level in 45 years, and mayors and governors regularly identify infrastructure quality and funding as among their most pressing problems. Eroding infrastructure threatens citizens' health, safety, and quality of life. Traffic congestion continues to grow, wasting time, fuel and causing unnecessary pollution. Water, critical for all life, is increasingly polluted, requiring expensive treatment. In addition, utility services, and Internet access and speed are necessary for modern commerce. As this is written, it is expected that there will be a large infusion of federal resources to repair, expand, and upgrade infrastructure. As discussed earlier, public funds are a critical piece of the puzzle, but there are also many opportunities for innovative approaches to finance that can leverage private sources of funding.

C. Chen and J. R. Bartle, *Innovative Infrastructure Finance*, https://doi.org/10.1007/978-3-030-91411-0_6

Chapter 2 identified three new challenges which call for new approaches to infrastructure development. First, natural disasters are occurring more frequently and are more severe, calling for improved protection for coastal areas, floodplains, and areas prone to wildfires, drought, and tornados. Second, new technology presents many opportunities to improve efficiency, safety, and to reduce pollution, but it can also be costly, and in some cases challenging to implement. State and local government planners and capital managers will need to incorporate these technologies in current and future systems. Third, recent demands to address social inequities are particularly relevant to infrastructure policy. Historic discrimination and explicitly racist, sexist, and ableist policies are part of the capital landscape of many American communities. Reversing these policies can be a major challenge in many cases, but this does not deny the urgency of the issue. In addition, the decision-making process in many governments needs to be more open to disadvantaged communities.

Chapter 3 discussed the traditional funding and financing infrastructure approaches, and Chapter 4 examined the advantages and disadvantages of different innovative financing alternatives. The many approaches provide a wide array of choices for any government. As discussed in these chapters, different financing tools are more appropriate in different circumstances, depending on timing, project size, the government's financial situation, and equity considerations. Following the benefits-received principle by matching capital expenses with appropriate revenue sources can make financing more financially sustainable and more equitable.

Chapter 5 provided in-depth examinations of six different financial innovations. These innovations range widely in both their capacity to raise funds and in their complexity. New sources of funding can bring the private and philanthropic sectors in as partners, reduce the financial pressure on taxpayers, and effectively complement traditional funding sources. Private sources of funds can often be mobilized much faster than the time it takes to approve new public funding, and some, like P3s, can facilitate faster completion of projects. GSS bonds are efficient conduits of low-cost borrowing that are attractive to certain new investors, and SIB loans can reduce risk and access funds at low-interest rates. Some long-term private investors find it attractive to invest in stable, inflation-resistant, long-term public investments such as toll roads. Joint development projects and P3s can enhance urban development by leveraging private sector capital and increase transit ridership. In addition to their specific benefits, these innovations stretch intergovernmental aid and loans, leverage private funds, and enable governments to accelerate project completion with greater flexibility. As with traditional financing, one size does not fit all; different sources of financing fit certain projects better than others, and public managers need to choose wisely. If the right options are selected, many of these advantages can be realized. We expect innovative infrastructure financing to continue to grow and become part of the landscape of public capital finance.

While the focus of this book has been on financing and developing new and existing infrastructure, a wise manager will consider first the need for new assets. With rapid economic changes, the old way of doing things may not be the best. For example, the global COVID-19 pandemic has raised the question for both public and private organizations whether they need as much office space as they have or if employees can continue to work from home. If new space is not needed or can be configured differently to accommodate employees in less space, significant long-run savings can be realized. On the other hand, social changes may well call for the development of new infrastructures, such as broader Internet access and smart city technology. Managers should be flexible and demonstrate to appropriators that they have carefully examined all the alternatives.

6.2 The Challenge of Innovation

New approaches to financing infrastructure present unique challenges and opportunities that involve financing, governance, and management. Some of the important lessons learned for innovators are as follows:

- First, innovations in infrastructure financing may require changes in state and local laws and administrative arrangements. Obtaining legislative approval to authorize the use of innovative infrastructure financing is a critical first step that is not always easy, but as the Chicago parking meter case showed, it is of critical importance. To win support, effective education of the public and legislators is necessary, as well as sufficient time to analyze the terms of the contract and the finances. Government managers need to explain the feasibility and benefits of innovative infrastructure financing to legislators and be open to a frank dialogue about alternative financing options.
- Second, innovative infrastructure financing strategies often involve complex financing techniques and engage various external financial partners and stakeholders. Effectively working with new partners is often required in these arrangements. Many government professionals need to strengthen their understanding of these techniques, as well as their capacity

to manage these financing alternatives so as not to be captive to concessionaires and vendors. Professional training in this area is available, and government finance professionals should seek out these opportunities. State governments may also need to provide technical advice to local governments about innovative infrastructure financing alternatives they facilitate, such as state bond banks.

- Third, state and local governments need to ensure transparency and accountability when using new financing methods. For instance, government managers often are required to—and usually should—engage and inform citizens in the process of project planning, selection, and funding. Managers should also provide clear explanations of innovative financing tools being considered. Simple fact sheets, FAQ documents, and examples of how other communities have used these tools can help improve public understanding. In addition, simplified reports about the progress of projects can be helpful. Public managers can effectively use their communication skills and interpersonal relationships to explain how innovation can help reshape communities for the future.
- Fourth, matching innovative financing with appropriate projects is challenging but potentially rewarding for public managers. The goal is not just to raise money to fund a project but to create a linkage between project benefits and revenues that will be financially and administratively sustainable for the long term. Managers should review the degree to which services are supported by appropriate revenue sources and share this with elected officials and the public, so any subsidy from the general coffers is clear. As many examples indicate, good projects with appropriate financing can enhance community wealth, safety, and sustainability. But the tools of financing are a means to an end, not an end in themselves. The nitty–gritty of finance is not for everyone, nor does it need to be. Change agents need to help political leaders and the public keep their "eye on the prize." The goal is to develop new assets for the community that can make life better.
- Fifth, try not to leave money on the table. Users that benefit from the services provided should pay the costs unless there is a compelling reason otherwise. Willing sponsors and donors should be identified and solicited. Grants from philanthropic organizations and other governments should be considered. Often one revenue source can leverage another, so even a small amount of revenue from a new source can make a difference. Keep up to date with what other governments and agencies are doing to identify opportunities to grow revenues.

- Finally, just as a skilled craftsman selects the right tool for the job and knows how to use it, selecting the right financial tool requires knowledge, experience, and skilled use of the tool. The art of the craft is to match revenues with the flow of benefits coming to the community. This can bring in new sources of funding that reduces the burden on taxpayers and achieves broader and more durable support.

6.3 Conclusion

While the challenges seem daunting, history reminds us of the remarkable innovations in infrastructure development in the U.S. and the central role of government. Canals funded by states opened many river cities to prosperous trade in the early part of the nineteenth century. The transcontinental railroad, with the support of federal land grants, opened the whole nation to national and international markets in the latter part of that century. The Wright brothers invented the airplane in 1903, and the nation continues to lead the world in the network of air transportation facilities. The Federal Aid Highway Act of 1921 provided states 50/50 matching funds to build a network of highways, leading to the most expansive highway system in the world. Federal projects initiated by NASA, a federal agency, opened space exploration, and facilitated the development of the aerospace industry. Finally, the Internet was primarily developed in the U.S. by the Defense Department. All these innovations required new public revenue sources, good management systems, and effective governance structures often involving all three levels of government. The government was a key actor in the invention, development, and provision of the nation's infrastructure. While modern challenges are different, they are not insurmountable.

Like so many elements of state and local government, innovation in infrastructure financing is not for the faint of heart. However, the importance of the challenges facing our communities demands a wise and determined approach. Finance is changing, presenting new alternatives and opportunities. This book has identified and illustrated several alternatives and demonstrated how they had been used to grow communities. We hope this book provides public managers with the tools and the insights they need to make their communities safer, more sustainable, and more prosperous.

Index

C. Chen and J. R. Bartle, *Innovative Infrastructure Finance*, https://doi.org/10.1007/978-3-030-91411-0

Y

CPSIA information can be obtained
at www.ICGtesting.com
Printed in the USA
LVHW080850070322
712805LV00004B/255

9 783030 914103